Expanding Life

IN THE CHRISTIAN FAITH
WITH JUNIOR HIGHS

Nancy B. Geyer, editor

THE SEABURY PRESS · NEW YORK

Expanding Life was prepared from materials developed under
the direction of Robert G. Nesbit at St. Mary's Episcopal Church,
Park Ridge, Illinois, and was produced under the auspices of the
Executive Council of the Episcopal Church.

Copyright © 1972 by The Seabury Press, Incorporated
ISBN: 0-8164-5697-6
Library of Congress Catalog Card Number: 75-189103
Design by Carol Basen
Printed in the United States of America

WHAT'S BETWEEN THESE COVERS?

Fifty Sessions for adult leaders to use in their work with junior highs

—these may be used

in a weekly class or group

in a summer camp setting

for a weekend conference

mixed in with other sessions

on a "unit" basis using
sessions from areas of
concern

PURPOSE   This material is designed to help junior highs expand their understanding of Christianity as a reality in a real world.

OUTLINE OF THE CONTENTS   Four basic areas of concern are covered, with a specific focus and number of sessions listed for each.

Introductory

This material is written with a definite bias. That bias is contained in the following statements:

1. The Christian Faith embodies a broad, profound, and vital understanding of God and man—and of the meaning of human history and man's destiny in relationship to God as Creator and Redeemer.
2. Effective Christian Education has an active faith aspect—the work of the Holy Spirit in the processes of human growth and development, even in adolescence.
3. Where adult leaders and junior highs are engaged in interaction, it is necessary that the adults respond appropriately to the growth processes in the young people.

Some Approaches to BOYS and GIRLS in Early Adolescence

WHAT TWELVES TO FOURTEENS ARE LIKE

They have had a dozen or so years of gathering knowledge and experience.

But they have limited information and experience in many areas of life.

They are CURIOUS about:
What makes people tick?
Why is the world the way it is?

They are moving toward an increasing sense of responsibility and away from security.

They are beginning to search for self-direction and moving away from adult authority.

They are rapidly growing persons in transition—restless, changeable— often uncertain of what they want or don't know.

They are looking for adult models with whom they can identify. (As often as possible provide *both* a man and a woman as adult leaders of a group.)

APPROPRIATE ADULT RESPONSES THAT BRIDGE THE GAP

Enable them to work with and build on what they already know.

Supply facts and information which they don't have.

Capitalize on this curiosity by providing some real facts, about real people and the real world. Apply Christian understanding of why people and life are the way they are.

Challenge them with subjects that are both intellectually and emotionally stretching and involving.
One sign that you are getting through is if some young people get a little "heated up."

Let them sample freedom with responsibility in the group.
Enable them to see the *real* consequences of choices.
Focus on decisions as being their decisions to make and to live with.

Respond openly to them where they are at a given time without expecting them to remain the same.

Be consistent: say openly what you think, believe, feel.
Share your faith, doubts, searchings.
Share your responses to issues as *yours* but not necessarily RIGHT for that reason.
Communicate that you take them and what you are doing together seriously.

Some How To's for ADULTS

1. Arrange chairs so that they are in a circle—close enough to provide a sense of being together as a group with no one left out. Be sure that the circle is expanded to include any latecomer.
2. From session to session, sit in different places yourself. Encourage this flexibility in the group.
3. Limit the amount of "lecturing" you do. Let the session materials do most of your talking for you. When you participate, try to concentrate on:
   —Providing facts that are unknown or misunderstood (specifically, facts about how the real world operates, or facts about what Christian theology has to say in a certain area);

—Asking questions. Your most valuable single role is to ask open-ended questions that call for a complete response, rather than a simple "yes" or "no." Start questions with "who-what-why-when-where or how."

4. Ask specific, meaningful, provocative questions that can be answered. Avoid vague questions. "For what reasons would *you* want to do such a thing?" is a better question than, "What principles are people using when they do such a thing?"

5. Focus on the personal rather than the impersonal. Talk about yourself and *encourage* the group to talk about themselves, their friends, their parents, their experiences.

6. Use newsprint. It's a very valuable aid. Use it to make notes of points raised by the group. Draw on it. List your own points on it. Don't expect the group to keep track on their own of a complicated discussion. Keep track of it with them on the newsprint.

7. See that the discussion bounces around. Address questions—in an easy way—to shy or silent students. Direct questions away from the steadily talkative students.

8. Keep the discussion moving. When it gets bogged down, summarize what has been said; then use a question to get things going again.

9. Work toward a sense of easy interaction with and between the group. Achieving interaction takes time. Doing the following will help:

—Sit as much as possible in the circle, as a member of the group. Doing so allows you to talk as an equal.

—Speak to your group as you would speak to your friends; that is, as if they were adult. Use your normal expressions and vocabulary. Use ideas or ways of approaching subjects pretty much as you do with adults. This will enable the group to think and respond in a more adult fashion.

—Keep your voice down and avoid a "professorial" tone. Speaking in a soft voice often has the effect of quieting down a noisy group. If you speak calmly and conversationally, the group will do the same.

—At times, when you wish to discuss a difficult subject in some depth, remove the chairs and have everybody sit on the floor, in a circle. This "campfire" setting can help.

—Be willing to share your own problems, doubts, or fears. Your group can't very well identify with you if you never share your own human situation. This doesn't involve sharing privileged information. It does mean saying "I just don't know," when in fact you don't really know. It means admitting that some things are hard for you to do or not do.

10. Communicate that you take seriously what is going on in the group. Share your belief that you are jointly engaged in a very important task. Let the group know it is not a task to be taken lightly or treated casually. Let the group know that you think the subject you are discussing together is a very important one.

11. One of your key jobs is to cause the group to think, work, worry about the focus issues in the course. If your approach to each subject is lukewarm, or the "milksop" approach, you will cancel out the effectiveness of the ideas. Work with the group to enable them to think these matters through. Do not be content with surface responses. Each session contains one or more issues of real impact—but the group will not feel that impact unless they struggle, and hard.

(As for supplies, practically all you'll need is some kind of reproducing machine and plenty of newsprint and grease pencils.)

TWO SESSIONS: (Session One is an opening session of 40 to 60 minutes. Session Two is a second session of 50 minutes.)

OBJECTIVES: *To begin to get to know each other as members of a group.*
To establish both participation and personal sharing as group standards.

Use sections A, B, C as appropriate in your situation, or construct a more suitable session for getting acquainted.

Session One (40 to 60 minutes):

Section A (10 minutes)

Introduce yourself and share the session objectives.
Divide the group into pairs. Pair each person, insofar as possible, with someone he or she does not know well. Include yourself. Use a group of three if necessary.
Ask the pairs to take five minutes to get better acquainted. Let them know that after five minutes each pair will join another pair and each person will have a turn introducing his or her partner to the other pair.
The groups of four have five minutes to make the introductions.

Section B (10 minutes)

Form new pairs. Get acquainted for five minutes. Have each person individually write on a small piece of paper three or four words or phrases that describe his or her partner. Have the partners share with each other (but not with others) what they have written and their reactions.

Section C, 1st part (10 minutes)

Form new pairs. Get acquainted for 2 or 3 minutes. Each pair is to decide on a question they would like to ask another pair.
Form groups of four. Ask and answer each other's questions.

Section C, 2nd part (10 minutes)

Bring the total group together. Have the pairs share the questions they asked but not the answers they received. List the questions on newsprint.
Ask the group: "Looking at these questions, how would you describe us as a total group?"

Section C, 3rd part (15 minutes)

Have any pairs who wish to, share the answers they gave to questions.
Ask the group: "Reflecting on the answers we gave to some of these questions, how would you describe us as a group?"

Session Two (50 minutes):

OBJECTIVE: *To enable the group to build agreements as to their objectives and how they would like to work together.*

This session works best for groups of nine to eighteen persons.
Give each person a felt-tipped marking pen and a half sheet of newsprint.
Have the group divide into small groups of three.
In 15 minutes each person has the task of interviewing the other two (and adding his or her own ideas), as follows:
With things in mind like your objectives, what you want to learn, what you don't want to discuss, *Person (a)* in each group asks: "What do we hope will happen in this group?"
With things like attendance, participation, discipline, etc., in mind, *Person (b)* asks: "How would we like to work with each other as members of this group?"
Person (c) asks: "How would we like our adult leaders to function with our group?" The responses that describe how the group members want the adults to act should be as specific as possible.
Each person briefly records the answers from his or her group of three on newsprint.
During this 15-minute period, the adult leaders are writing on a sheet of newsprint their responses to: "How would we like to function in this group?"
After 15 minutes—or sooner if the groups of three have completed their task—have all the "a's" meet together, all the "b's," all the "c's."
Each new group has 10 minutes to build one list on a sheet of newsprint that combines the points made in the groups of three. They do not duplicate or omit. If there are contradictory points, all should be written down.
Have the total group gather in a circle. Post the combined list from subgroup "a."
Make needed clarifications and decisions between any suggestions that are contradictory.

Repeat with the reports from group "b" and group "c."

After group "c" reports, have the adult leaders post their sheet and have the total group compare the two. Look for similarities. Discuss and negotiate any differences.

After the session these sheets can be rewritten on newsprint (making a combination of the youth-adult reports on how the leaders will function) and permanently posted in the group's room.

Sheet a headed—Group Objectives

Sheet b headed—Our Contract with Each Other as Group Members

Sheet c headed—Our Contract with our Group Leaders

Every five or six sessions the group needs to evaluate its life against these sheets, either improving the contracts themselves *or* changing how they are working as a group to bring what they are experiencing more in line with the contracts.

Take 15 minutes at the end of a session and have the group discuss:

How are we doing in relation to our objectives and our contracts?

What would we like to do differently?

Personal Values and Morality

One Session (50 minutes):

OBJECTIVES: *To help the group discover:*
  (a) *When persons play life as a game there is no wholly satisfactory or successful strategy for "winning";*
  (b) *That Christianity does not view life as a game to be won.*

Hand out to each group member a copy of the sheet headed GAMESMANSHIP (page 16). Have someone read it through aloud with the rest of the group following.

Discuss the following questions:

What do you think about the idea of being a *"shark"*?

Who encourages you to play life as a game in that way?

What weaknesses are there in this approach?

What about being an *"expert"*?

What's wrong with that approach?

Does anyone ever play "expert"? Who? When and where?

How useful is it to be a *"psychologist"*?

What's wrong with just "playing the people"?

What about being a *"plunger"*? Anything wrong with that?

How about the reverse—being a *"fraidycat"*?

Would you be willing to be a *"dumbbell"*? Why not?

What in playing life as a game is the equivalent of a *kibitzer* in a card game?

If you really wanted to win in a card game, what guaranteed method could you use for winning? (answer: cheating.)

Can we agree on which of these strategies is the best of all?

Why is it so difficult to agree on the best strategy?

What does Christianity say about playing life as a game?

How many people do you know who say they believe what Christianity has to say about life who still play life like a card game to be won? Why do you think this is so?

If life were a card game like poker or bridge, which of the following ways would you play it?

THE SHARK

Really get *good* at the game. Learn to keep track of how the cards are played, know who is holding what cards, know how best to play your own cards. Learn the art and science of the game.

THE EXPERT

Memorize every rule, since most people play the game just for fun. This way you can win by enforcing each little rule they forget or ignore.

THE PSYCHOLOGIST

Play the people, not just the cards. Bluff, hold back, fake out the other players. Get to know the strengths and weaknesses of each player, and change your tactics accordingly.

THE PLUNGER

Go for broke. Bet high, force as many people to chicken out as you can. Either win big, or lose big.

THE FRAIDYCAT

Play your cards very carefully. Don't risk too much, except on sure things. Pass whenever it doesn't look as though there's much chance of winning. Don't figure on winning much, just make sure you don't lose much either.

THE DUMBBELL

Play the game for fun. Don't worry too much how well you do, and don't try too hard. The other players will like you better—and they'll always want you to sit in.

THE KIBITZER

Don't really play the game. It's more fun—and less dangerous—to stand on the sidelines and criticize what the other players do.

One Session (45 minutes)

OBJECTIVE:

(a) *To expand the group's understanding of some of the bases on which people may be judged guilty.*

(b) *To look at some reasons why individuals may or may not repent.*

Explain to the group that during this session you will be talking about two things: first about guilt; second about people being sorry for things they have done wrong.

Hand out pencils and copies of SHEET A (page 18) to each member of the group. Have someone read the descriptions aloud.

Ask everyone to rank each person described by putting *1st Worst* next to the description of the person they personally believe is most guilty of wrongdoing; *2nd Worst* by the person next in guilt; *3rd Worst* by the one they think is least guilty.

On a newsprint chart put all three names and the votes they received, for example as follows:

	1st Worst	*2nd Worst*	*3rd Worst*
Himmler	〣〣 (5)	// (2)	/ (1)
Jones	// (2)	〣〣/ (6)	
Withers	/ (1)	// (2)	〣〣 (5)

1. Have the group share and discuss the reasons for their ratings.

2. Ask: "What do the reasons we gave tell us about the ways we judge people as guilty?"

3. If no one rated Marion Withers 1st or 2nd, ask: "Can you conceive of any reason for Marion being first or second? If so, why? If not, why not?"

Again ask them to rank 1st, 2nd, 3rd each description in response to this question:

"Which of these three people would you suppose is actually aware of doing something wrong? (Which do you suppose is most likely to feel sorry?)"

1st—most likely to repent

2nd—next most likely to repent

3rd—least likely to repent

1. Again post the results on newsprint and have the group share and discuss their reasons for their ratings.

2. What have we learned about what is likely to cause people to be sorry?

HEINRICH HIMMLER headed the Gestapo in Nazi Germany. He was a cold, unemotional individual. He was seldom heard to shout and, so far as is known, never committed a personally violent act. (As a matter of fact, the sight of blood made him feel squeamish.) All that he ever did was to sit at a desk and quietly and efficiently administer the execution of roughly six million people.

SAM JONES is often drunk. He has never held a job more than two weeks, and he makes most of his living through petty thievery. One day when he comes home drunk, his wife criticizes him, and he beats her into unconsciousness.

MARION WITHERS is thirteen years old. She is polite, quiet, and a good student. She is also forgetful. After she loses her best coat (for the second time) her mother says, "Marion, that's the last straw. You can just cancel your plans for this weekend. You're staying in the house." Marion says nothing, but goes to her room. For long moments she stares at herself in the mirror. She has only one thought: "I wish my mother would die."

FOCUS: CHEATING

Two Sessions (each 45 minutes)

The sessions should be used in sequence.

Session One:

OBJECTIVES: *To have each group member:*
  (a) *Make conscious public choices;*
  (b) *Reflect upon the implications of those choices;*
  (c) *Consider some possible consequences of those choices.*

Share the focus of the session with the group and give each person a sheet that reproduces THE EXAM—SESSION ONE (page 20). Have someone read it aloud with the rest of the group following. Allow 3 to 5 minutes for each person to mark his or her choices.

Record all answers on a newsprint chart as follows:

	1st choice	2nd choice	3rd choice	4th choice
Go.				
Stay and say nothing.				
Stay and tell your friend to stay.				
Stay and tell your friend you'll help.				

Discuss each first choice asking:

"Why would you be most likely to do this?"

"What do your reasons tell you about what is most important to you in this situation?"

Discuss each fourth choice asking the same two questions.

Discuss each of the four choices asking:

"What would be the possible consequences of that choice?"

"How do you feel about those consequences?"

"If those consequences occurred, how satisfied would you be with your choice?"

"What do your feelings say about what is most important to you in this situation?"

If time allows, ask: "What would you do if you believed that neither you nor your friend could pass the exam? Would this affect the order of your choices?"

"If so ,what would the changes be?"

"For what reasons would you make those changes?"

"What do your reasons say to you about your values in this situation?"

Session Two:

OBJECTIVE: *To allow group members to explore:*
  (a) *Some of the meanings of different verbal responses they might make under the pressure of being told by someone that what they are doing is cheating;*
  (b) *Some of the more basic implications of cheating in everyday life.*

Tell the group you are going to continue with your discussion of cheating, but that you will be looking at it from a different angle.

Hand out pencils and the sheet THE EXAM—SESSION TWO (page 21). Read it through aloud. Allow group members three minutes to check their responses.

List the responses on newsprint. Have a show of hands of how many checked each one and post the results beside each response. Add other responses that group members wrote down.

Take each response, beginning with the one receiving the most checks. Ask about each:

"What are we *really saying* when we make this response?"

or

"What does this response *really mean?*"

After discussing each response ask:

"What would be the hardest response to make? Why?"

"Reflecting on our discussion, what would you say our feelings about being accused of cheating are?"

"What do you see as our general attitudes and feelings about cheating in this situation?"

"Where do you see cheating going on in everyday life?"

"What are the basic problems that cheating in any area of life can cause?"

THE EXAM—SESSION ONE

You and your best friend are studying for a crucial exam in a required course. The exam is tomorrow. If you don't pass the exam with a good grade, you will fail the course and have to repeat it. Your friend is in the same situation.

The phone rings. It is a third friend who joyfully tells you, "I've got a copy of the examination. Come on over!"

At this point you are sure you can pass the exam, but you are equally sure your friend can't.

What would you be most likely to do:

Go.	Stay and say nothing to your friend about the call.	Stay and tell your friend not to go either.	Stay and say you will try to help your friend study.

Using the numbers 1, 2, 3, 4, with 1 standing for what you would be *most* likely to do and 4 standing for your least likely choice, assign a number to each alternative.

Give your honest personal opinion.

THE EXAM—SESSION TWO

You and your best friend are studying for a crucial final exam in a required course. The exam is tomorrow. If you don't pass the exam with a good grade, you will fail the course and have to repeat it. Your friend is in the same situation.

The phone rings. It is a third friend who joyfully announces, "I've got a copy of the examination. Come on over!"

At this point, you feel sure there is no way for you to pass the exam. Your friend claims to be certain of passing. Since you are desperate, you decide to go. Which of the following things would you be most likely to say if your friend told you: "I don't think you should go. That would be cheating." *Check all of the statements you might make, not just one.* Add any others below.

—"How come you're so sure you can pass, anyway?"

—"Listen, what I do is none of your business."

—"No, I'm going anyway!"

—"O.K., I'll stay, but you've got to work with me."

—"O.K., you're right. I'll stay."

_____

_____

_____

One to Two Sessions (45 minutes each):

OBJECTIVE: *To explore the issue of children rejecting their parents.*

1. Give each member of the group a copy of THE KING'S CHOICE—PART I (page 23) and have one person read aloud while the rest listen.

2. Ask the group:
   (a) "What are your reactions to the king's decision to choose as ruler the child who acted most as he did? Why do you feel as you do?"
   (b) "In this situation how do you predict each of the children will react and why? Alpha? Marianne? Elizabeth?"

3. Distribute THE KING'S CHOICE—PART II (page 24) and ask someone to read it aloud while the others listen.

4. Ask the group:
   (a) If the king had to make a choice now, what do you think he would do? Why?
   (b) The king says his children are rejecting him. Do you agree? Why or why not?
   (c) Do these children and their father remind you of anyone? If so, who?
   (d) Do you think your parents act or feel like the king in the story did? How? Why?
   (e) Do you ever see yourself responding to your parents as any of the king's children did to him? How? Why?
   (f) What would help parents and children better handle these situations when they occur?
   (g) What relationships do you see between the reaction of these children to their father, and the way many people react to God?

Once upon a time, there was a wise and powerful king, the ruler of a mighty empire. Many years before, when he had assumed the throne, his nation had been a struggling little kingdom, beset by enemies on all sides.

But over a time the king conquered his enemies, brought peace and prosperity to the land, and was generally regarded as the greatest ruler in those parts.

Now the king was growing older. Although still a vigorous and strong man, he realized he could not live forever, and so he began to make plans for the future.

His most important decision revolved around the choice of a future ruler. He had three children, and one of them must be chosen to be the new ruler and be prepared for that important position.

As he considered his children, the king could not discern any real differences between them; at least not in terms that would make his choice any easier.

Alpha, the oldest, was an exceedingly intelligent, handsome boy. He was a born student, although he was also a vigorous hunter and fighter—an excellent combination in a ruler, the king thought. On the other hand, Alpha was inclined to be overly selfish; overly concerned with getting his own way; sometimes unfair to others in his struggles to win various contests.

Marianne was the second child and in many ways the delight of her father. She was a bright, quick, and a superbly graceful individual. A beauty to behold. But Marianne's most marked characteristic was an ingrained gentleness; a sensitivity to the feelings of others; a desire to maintain peace and tranquility; a sereneness; a desire to serve. Everyone loved Marianne, just as everyone was a bit awed by Alpha. Here, too, though, the king could see certain flaws. Sometimes, in her efforts to smooth over things, Marianne would give in too readily. (It is true that at times she would lose her temper, but that was not really her way.) Would Marianne perhaps be too eager to please; too eager to do what others wanted, to the possible detriment of the kingdom?

Elizabeth was the youngest and by all odds the most interesting and complex of the three. Being the third child, she had always had to struggle for the attention and affection of her father. In the process, she had acquired a most amazing capacity to fascinate and delight others. Elizabeth could, when the occasion demanded, be as headstrong as Alpha, at other times as gentle and caring as Marianne. Possessing neither the native intelligence or physical looks of her brother and sister, Elizabeth exceeded them both in sheer ingenuity. Alpha could get his way through ability. Marianne might get her way because people could not help but love her. Elizabeth got her way by whatever strategem was necessary. She was sly and quick. And if at times she caused her father concern, she spent most of the time causing him intense happiness. A ruler must know how to cope, and Elizabeth was a real coper. On the other hand, thought the king, might Elizabeth be too inclined to live by expedience rather than principle? Might she act in the way that produced results rather than in the way that is right?

The king continued to ponder. "Alpha has the greatest natural ability," he thought. "But Marianne has the most concern for others." But again, "Elizabeth is the quickest; the most flexible." "Whom shall I choose?"

The king met with his councillors. After much thought and discussion, they hit upon a scheme. "Whatever the capabilities of your children may be," said the king's advisers, "the fact remains that the best qualified person is the person most able to act like you. You are the model for a new ruler. Therefore, the child who is most able to emulate you—to act as you have acted—must be the choice."

And so the king met with his children and told them of the decision. The future ruler would be the one who most acted as he did. The king assured his children that they would all make most excellent rulers, but still some choice had to be made.

How disappointed the king was in the days that followed!

Alpha went into a rage. He stated that such a system was impossible. He said it was unfair. Privately, to himself, he said, "I am a better man than my father." And, finally, Alpha left the kingdom to set up his own nation.

Marianne bowed her head and admitted, "It will be terribly difficult to act like you, but I will try." The king was very pleased, of course, but it quickly became apparent that Marianne did not really mean what she had said. Although she remained a loyal and affectionate daughter at all times, she continued to be what she had always been. She simply never changed, and she seemed to count on the fact of her goodwill toward her father to win her the position.

Elizabeth at first said nothing. She was grateful that Alpha had departed, for she knew that in a real contest of wills Alpha would win out. That left her with Marianne to contend with. For a time, it seemed for all the world that Elizabeth would win out. She did begin to style her behavior after her father. But the king discovered one day that Elizabeth had not really tried to change. He came upon Elizabeth engaged in an argument with Marianne, calling her sister every name in the books, telling her she was weak and stupid. Poor Marianne was saying nothing, trying to keep the peace. Badgering someone was something the king would never do, he told himself, and he knew then that recently Elizabeth had only been acting a part.

And so the king sent each of his children a letter. In the letter he expressed his disappointment. He said to them, "I want to give you everything I have. But, for your own good, you must each try to become something more than you are. Each, in your own way, has rejected me. Why is this? The experience of years shows clearly that copying me is the path to what each of you wants, yet you insist on going your own way. Each of you has great capability and need change only a little. Why will you not make any attempt to change?"

He got his replies:

Alpha said, " I want no part of you. I am as capable as you are, and I refuse to bend myself to anyone's will. I am independent, and I will make my own way and be my own person."

Marianne said, "I cannot do what you want. I have tried, and it does not seem right to me. Please forgive me. I am doing what I can, but I remain what I am."

Elizabeth said, "But I have done what you wanted. I acted the way you wanted me to act. Why then must you pry into my motives? My reasons are my own. If I follow your rules, that is all you have a right to ask for."

One Session (45 minutes):

OBJECTIVES: *To help group members:*
(a) *really feel how it is to be somebody else;*
(b) *to write a prayer of supplication.*

Appropriate timing is important if this session is to be effective. Use it when the group is rather pensive (not when they are bright or uproarious).

Introduce the session by describing the experience. If the following is true of your class, you might comment that whether they always recognize it or not, they are very lucky people, living in a prosperous community and looking forward to limitless possibilities in the future. Whether this is the case for your particular group or not, most young people are naturally optimistic. There is no denying the fact that people's lives do not always turn out the way they expect them to. This is particularly true for some of the people in our society. For them, life is not at all the way your group may experience it.

Today, they are going to have a chance to find out something of how it feels to not have things turn out the way you expect when you are young.

Explain that you are going to give to each of them a situation. The girls will get a situation about a woman. The boys will get one about a man. Both the man and the woman are older than they are, but they can imagine that they are these people. Confidential note to the leader: One of the primary developmental tasks of young people of these ages is identification with persons of their own sex.

The situations are not complete. Their job is to make them complete. Each person is to do this by writing, for one of these two people, a prayer. It may be a short prayer, but they may find they are able to write a rather long prayer. They are to write it as if they were one of the people they are going to read about.

Explain that they are not to talk while they are reading and writing. It will help to play a record while they read and write. Pick some quiet background music.

Let the group work as long as they wish on this exercise. You may not want to talk about it until the next session.

When you do talk about it, have each member read what he or she has written. Or, have all the students exchange papers and let them read somebody else's work. Both case situations should be read aloud at this point so that everyone is familiar with both stories.

HOW IT ALL TURNED OUT FOR HER

It is getting dark in your one-room apartment, but it saves money not to turn on the light. There is no television, no telephone, and no books save a shabby Bible. You have just finished eating your supper of bean soup and tea.

It is dusk outside. Looking out the window you can see several small, dirty children playing leapfrog over the garbage cans lying in the street. In a doorway across the street a young man is talking to a girl. They seem to be sharing a lovely secret.

You think back to that long-ago day when you first met your husband. How strong he was, how vigorous! He had this warm, wonderful, masculine laugh. It seemed there was nothing he couldn't do, or at least that he wouldn't try.

You even remember your wedding. Oh, your folks couldn't afford much, but, my, what a good time everyone had. And how beautiful you looked in your wedding gown. You almost forgot it was second-hand.

It had been so good, so very good for those first few years in the spring of your life. Your husband had a good job. But something had happened. Hard times? Bad luck? Who can tell? Somehow he aged before his time. Got discouraged, old, embittered; snarled at "the system," or "that lousy boss."

Then came the two children, lovely girls, but way too expensive. It had been too much. Why did he have to leave? Surely, you could have made out somehow. One day, he just went to the door and never came back.

The girls missed him—but not the way you did. They never knew him the way he had been—the way you knew him. It all just left an empty spot inside you, never filled.

Now? Well, one day goes on to the next. It is, after all, not a bad job—cooking for somebody else. The lady has an awfully nice house, and she isn't so bad to work for. Oh, she gets a little snippy every now and then, especially when her husband goes on those long business trips. (But then, he has an important job.) Anyway, it's a job.

"Funny," you say aloud. "You'd think one of the girls would come back." You remember now, it's been three years since you saw the younger one. "I wish there'd been more time to spend with them," you think. "They were nice girls—once."

It is getting chilly, and your apartment has no heat. It's still October, and the landlord won't provide heat until November. "In a way," you muse, "life is like a year. It's sure late autumn for me. Well, even so, summer wasn't so good either. Maybe winter will bring happier times. Maybe." Your legs are awfully tired from standing all day. You sit down in your one chair, lean back and close your eyes. Almost without willing it, you find a prayer coming to your lips. YOU SAY . . .

HOW IT ALL TURNED OUT FOR HIM

Once, a long, long time ago you were really a cool cat. Sharp clothes, ready money, your choice of any girl. Those had been good times.

Ah, and your best girl. She was really something. Quick on the trigger, a gorgeous figure—everything.

And so you married her. At first, things had really hummed along. Those were good times, and it was easy to make money. You took a job when you needed it, and you spent whatever you made. You and she had sure lived the life then.

Whatever happened, anyway? How is it that you're strong and young one day—old and tired the next? How can just ten years make such a difference?

"Boy, my legs hurt," you think. "Been walking all day trying to get a job, and nobody'll hardly even talk to me." Most of the men were polite but firm: "Sorry fellow, we just don't have any openings. You know how it is."

One of them did go on, though. He told you, "No, son, I don't think I could take the risk. You never held down any jobs before. You'd probably just leave me, the way you left everybody else."

"But this time I need work," you replied. "I mean, I've got to have money. Look, I'll do anything, I don't care. I can't afford to quit."

"I know," the man said, "that's how it is till you get a little dough in your pocket. Then you'll up and quit. Nope, I'm sorry, but I just don't want to take the chance."

You wish now you hadn't told the guy off. He sure deserved it, though. He ought to step in your shoes sometime. You've got just $50.00 left. The $100.00 rent on your apartment is due in five days, and if you don't pay, out you go—you and your wife and the three kids. And those kids. Why, they're living on a diet of thinned rice soup and water right now.

And your wife. Not pretty anymore. Not bright. Just tired—and looking twenty years older than she is.

It makes your skin crawl when you think about something she said to you on your wedding day, ten years ago: "You're my man," she said. "You're a real man who can lick the world; who can take care of me."

"Lord," you wonder, "would the loan company come up with just a couple of hundred dollars or so?" No, there's no way that will happen. Your wife has been locking the door and making the kids keep quiet anyway, so the bill collectors won't know anybody's home.

"Maybe what I oughta do is just take off," you consider. "There's got to be more to life than this."

You are just a few blocks now from your apartment. Your wife and kids are waiting, hoping for good news, just this once. It is almost dark. You pass by the open door of a shabby little store-front church. It looks so cool, so nice and dark and peaceful in there that you just can't help walking in. "Just to check out the joint," you say to yourself.

"I am tired," you think. "Maybe if I just sit down here a minute, I'll feel better." And so you do. Up in front, sitting on a cloth-covered card table that substitutes for an altar, there is a small wooden cross.

Half joking, half serious, you address that cross. "Jesus, let me tell you something . . ."

One Session (45 minutes):

OBJECTIVE: *To deepen the group members' understanding of the concept of brotherly love.*

1. Ask the group what "the summary of the law" is.
2. Ask what they think the part, "Thou shalt love thy neighbor as thyself," really means.
3. Distribute pictures A through F, and have the group read through the text that goes with them.
4. Have the group divide into six teams—one for each picture—and give each team five minutes to write a one-paragraph description of what they think their picture means.
5. Each team reads its definition, beginning with picture A. After each description is read, have the group discuss the principles involved in each picture and give examples of the principles they see.
6. Distribute picture G. Have group as a whole discuss its meaning and examples of it.

This is a couple who know they love their fellow man. Color them confident.

They enjoy the good things in life (and that helps them love themselves, too). Color them prosperous.

In fact, they are so pleased with themselves, they have decided that those other people (whom they love so much) would be a lot better off if they were more like them. Color them superior.

Hey, some of those other people are saying, "We don't want to be like you." Color them offended.

They have noticed that some of those other people aren't like them *at all*. They look strange; they dress strangely; they want strange things. They want to *change* things. Color them worried.

They wish very much that some awful thing would happen to those other people. Color them hateful.

They just left church, where they heard the nicest sermon on brotherly love. Color them confident again.

Four Sessions (45 minutes each):

OBJECTIVE: *To have group members learn how they may achieve greater self-awareness through reflection and self-examination.*

INTRODUCTION: These sessions provide an opportunity for individual reflection and self-examination. They would be appropriate as a series of consecutive weekly sessions or in a conference setting during the Lenten season.

Session One:

1. Share the objective for the sessions, and hand out copies of Mirror #1 (page 31).
2. Ask the group to help you build a newsprint list of things they know or could easily find out about themselves and others. Included could be:
   —name, address, age
   —occupation
   —performance in school
   —what you like to do
   —what you don't like to do
   —what you are good at, and not good at
3. One way to do some self-examination is to think about our individual answers to questions like those. Ask them to write down individually their responses in their mirror. Make a list for yourself also. Explain that they do not have to share what they write unless they choose to.
4. Allow all the time needed for the lists; if there is any time left, ask volunteers to read an item or two from their mirrors.
5. Ask: "Did what you wrote describe everything about you?" The obvious answer is no. Explain that in the next session you will work with another area of self-awareness.
   Ask them to keep their mirrors.

Session Two:

1. Review briefly what happened in the last session.
2. Hand out copies of Mirror #2. Explain that when they write their answers for this mirror they are only *guessing*. If they knew for sure, the answers would be in Mirror #1. This time they will *not* discuss *what* they wrote, but there will be general discussion after everyone has a chance to write some guesses.
3. Ask them to put their mirrors away while you discuss:
   (a) "Is this kind of self-examination important? Why? Why not?"

(b) "In what ways might you get a clearer, more accurate picture of what is in this second mirror?"
Possible responses may include paying greater attention to how others respond to you; listening; asking others directly how they see you in a specific area about which you would like to know more.
4. Explain there are still other kinds of self-examination and that the next session they will work with a different mirror.

Session Three:

1. Review briefly the last two sessions.
2. Distribute Mirror #3. Explain that there will be *no* sharing with anyone else what each person writes.
3. Allow all the time needed for writing. Then ask the group to put their mirrors away.
4. Have a general discussion of questions like these:
   (a) "Is this a helpful kind of self-examination? Why? Why not?"
   (b) "What sorts of things do people hide from others?"
   (c) "Is what we have done a complete self-examination? Why? If not—what else is there?"

Session Four:

1. Review the discussion of (c) under (4) in the last session.
2. Hand out Mirror #4. Have the class discuss the question, "Is there anything in it?" One kind of answer is that all of a person's God-given but undeveloped potential is there.
   Ask the group if that is a possibility for the content of this mirror—then:
   "How important is this mirror?"
   "What can be done about what's in it?"
3. Summarize the approach you have taken to self-examination by showing on newsprint all four mirrors together, making a complete picture of one way of describing what a person is and one way of having a person examine himself or herself for greater self-awareness.
4. Ask:
   (a) "What have you liked or not liked about this approach to achieving increased self-awareness?"
   (b) "Reflecting on our answers to (a), what can we see about ourselves as a group?"

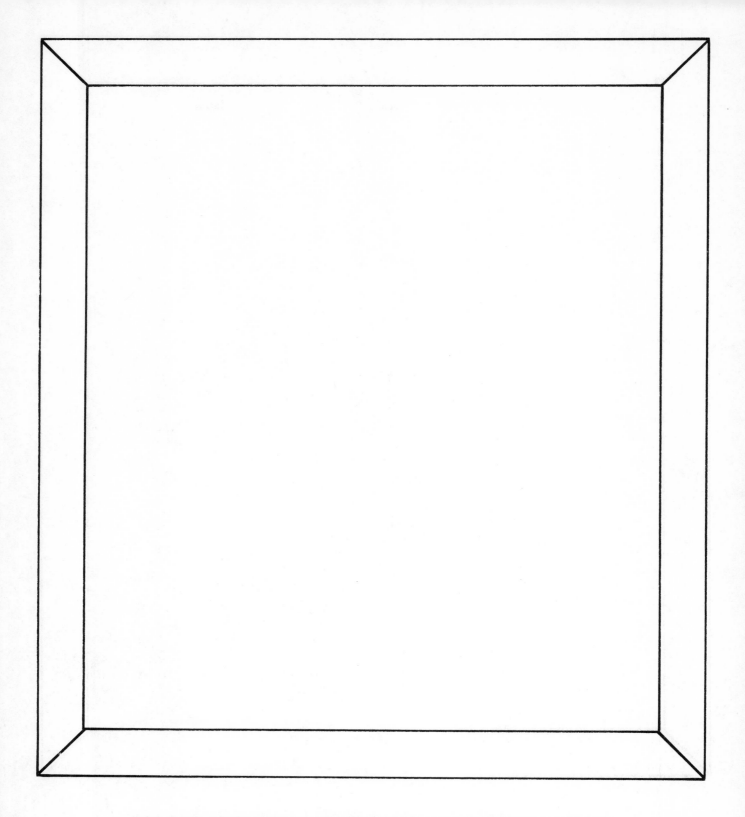

THIS IS THE MIRROR THAT REFLECTS THINGS EVERYBODY KNOWS ABOUT YOU—AND THAT YOU KNOW ABOUT YOURSELF. IT SHOWS THE SAME PICTURE TO YOU AND OTHER PEOPLE.

WHAT IS IN THIS MIRROR?

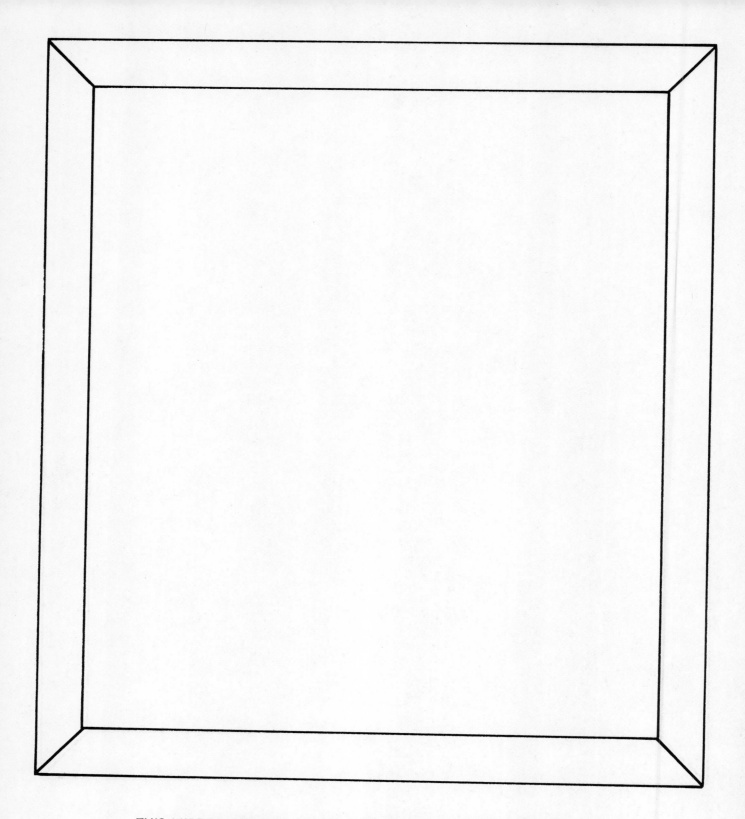

THIS MIRROR REFLECTS THINGS ABOUT YOU, BUT ONLY OTHER PEOPLE CAN SEE IT. THAT IS, IT REFLECTS HOW OTHERS SEE YOU, BUT ONLY THE THINGS YOU *CANNOT* SEE.

WHAT DO YOU SUPPOSE IT SHOWS?

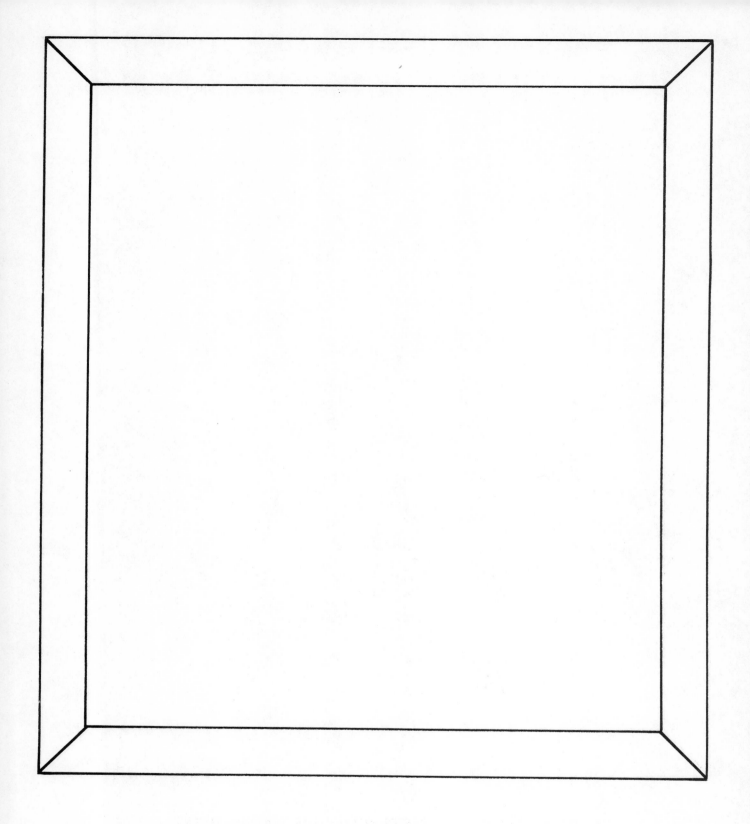

NO ONE EXCEPT YOU SEES ANYTHING IN THIS MIRROR. IT REFLECTS THE THINGS ABOUT YOU THAT OTHERS DON'T KNOW ABOUT.

WHAT DOES IT SHOW?

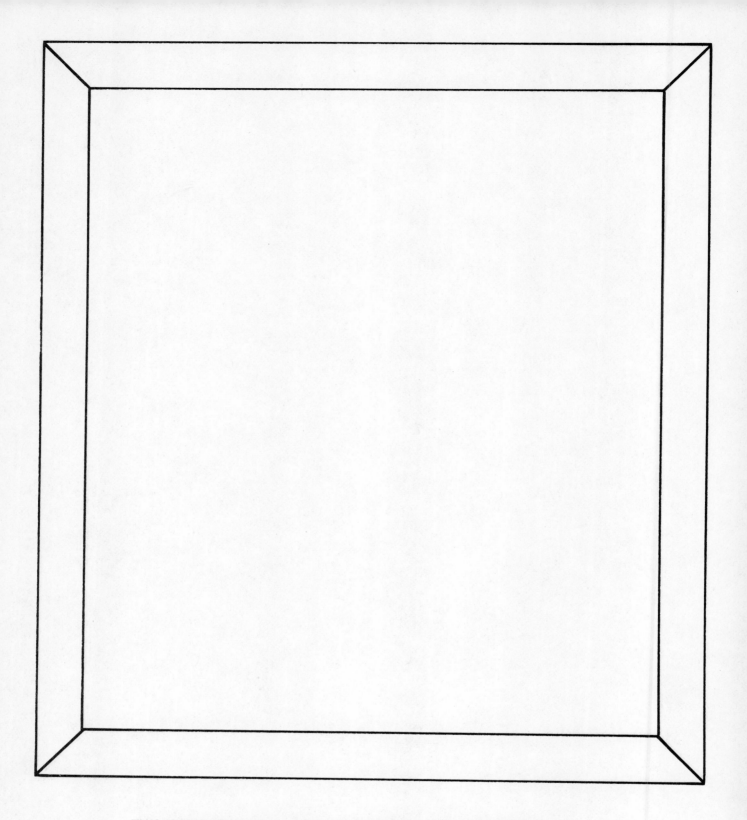

THIS IS THE MIRROR NOBODY SEES INTO, EITHER YOU OR OTHERS.
IS THERE *ANYTHING* IN IT? IF SO, WHAT?

In using the sections of this series on life goals it is important to follow the sequence suggested. However, the sessions are best used over a period of time with other sessions intermixed. For example, if you are using this material on a weekly basis, devote one session to this focus, then skip two or three weeks before returning to the subject. You will need to spend about fourteen sessions in all.

Section A—Two Sessions (40 minutes each):

OBJECTIVES: *To enable the group to:*
    (a) *consciously think about specific goals they can and will pursue in their lives;*
    (b) *decide for themselves the relative importance of these goals.*

Session One:

Give each group member the handout WHAT ARE YOU AFTER? (page 36). Go over the instructions together and ask everyone to rank the list of goals. Rank a list yourself. Working on the lists may take most of one session.

At the end of the session ask each member of the group to mark "Y" (for Youth) in the top right-hand corner of his or her sheet.

Give each person two additional WHAT ARE YOU AFTER? handouts and ask them to have their parents complete them. (Some of your students may have only one parent at home or may not live with a parent at all. They might ask other adults who are close to them to complete the handouts.) Ask the group to bring the completed handouts next time you meet. If you are using this material in a conference setting, ask them to have the handouts completed by other adults who are there.

After collecting the handouts completed by the adults, and BEFORE Session 2, do the following:
—Make sure adult and youth handouts are kept separate.
—Tabulate the rankings on two newsprint charts, one for the young people and one for the adults. This is done as follows:
    —Add up the numbers given by the young people to each of the twelve possible life goals and record the totals. Do the same for the adults.
    —Divide the total for each life goal by the number of persons who ranked that goal. This gives you an

"average priority ranking" for each goal. (If any average priority rankings involve fractions, round them off to the nearest whole number.) Repeat for the adults.
—When you have finished these calculations, make up two newsprint charts as shown below—one for youth rankings and another for adult rankings, including your own.

SAMPLE CHART—RELATIVE IMPORTANCE
GIVEN TO TWELVE LIFE GOALS

Each goal is an abbreviated version of the longer definitions provided on the handout, "What Are You After?" The figures are hypothetical.

Life Goals	Average Priority Ranking Youth
Survival	3
Security	2
Ease	6
Friendship	7
Affluence	1
Prestige, respect	5
Achievement	4
Knowledge	12
Use of abilities (or growth)	9
Peace of mind	8
Love	11
Go to Heaven	10

Session Two:

Share the two charts. Using one life goal as an example, explain how you arrived at the numbers.

Discuss the following three areas for *each goal*—comparing what the youth said and what the adults said for that goal.
    (a) Why they think the adults rated it as they did.
    (b) Why they think the young people rated it as they did.
    (c) What the group members see as the significance of the difference in priority between youth and adults.

WHAT ARE YOU AFTER?

A series of twelve possible purposes or goals in life is listed below. Your job is to rank them in order of their importance to you. Give a rank of "12" to the personal goal you consider most important, "11" to the next most important goal, and so on down to "1" for the goal you personally consider least important.

Be as honest as possible. Don't rank a goal high if it isn't really important to you or just because you think people *should* have it as a high goal. These rankings are what *you* really think.

If it is difficult to decide just what the order of importance is for you, give two or more goals the same rating. For example, you might give two different goals the number "8" because they are equally important to you. If you do so, however, *then skip the next number.* For example, if you give two goals an "8" then skip "7" and give the next most important goal a "6." Or, if you assign an "8" to three different goals, then skip both the "7" and the "6" and give your next most important goal a "5."

My goals in life are to:
—Stay alive as long as possible, and avoid pain and discomfort.
—Be as secure as possible; keep what I have and avoid unpleasant surprises.
—Live an easy life, not working too hard or undergoing too much stress and strain.
—Have a lot of friends.
—Own a lot of nice things; have a high standard of living.
—Be respected for what I am and what I accomplish.
—Get a lot of things done; work hard and well and accomplish something important.
—Know a lot—be smart, well educated, wise, etc.
—Make the most of myself; use whatever talents I was born with, and use them to the utmost.
—Enjoy real peace of mind; not worry too much, and feel life is good.
—Be loved by other people, or at least a few other people.
—Go to heaven and live eternally.

DO NOT SIGN YOUR NAME

Section B—Twelve Sessions (30 minutes each, except for the first session which will take longer):

OBJECTIVE: *To enable the group to look at how well a certain life style will work to achieve a specific life goal.*

Each session works further with one of the twelve life goals in Section A. To start the first session in this section, distribute the handout "Your Options in Life" (page 38) and discuss the options for understanding. Do *not* try to connect these options with life goals yet.

Beginning with the life goal that received the highest priority from the youth, take the following steps:

1. Give each group member a copy of the options handout and have them, working on their own, rank the options "5" to "1" in terms of how effective they feel each option would be in pursuing the particular life goal you are discussing in that session. The rank of "5" should be given to the life-style option they feel would be best in achieving that life goal; "1" should be given to the option they feel would be least effective in achieving that life goal.

2. Make a newsprint chart (an example is shown below). Tally the number of "5's," "4's," etc. Total as shown.

3. Discuss the question: "What are our reactions to the life-style priority ranking we have in relation to this goal?"

Life Goal: Achievement						
Styles	5's	4's	3's	2's	1's	*Total*
Self	(25)	(24)	(9)	(4)	(1)	63
Group	(15)	(24)	(9)	(6)	(4)	58
Expediency	(35)	(12)	(15)	(6)	(1)	69
Others	(5)	(8)	(12)	(10)	(5)	40
Christianity	(5)		(6)	(8)	(6)	25

*The "TOTAL" equals the number of votes in each column multiplied by the value of that column. For example, 5 votes in the "5's" column equals a total of 25.

NOTE: Keep all twelve goal charts with the point totals. You will need these in section C.

While there are many possible ways to live your life, it simplifies things to boil them down to a few broad "options." Some of these options are listed below.

1. *Do what you want to do,* for whatever reasons you want to do it. Live "according to your own lights," to satisfy your own needs and wants, not what anybody else wants or what somebody says you "ought to" do.

2. *Live according to what the people you know say is right,* or what some particular *group to which you belong says is right.* For instance, if you consider yourself to be an "upper middle class American," then this option would mean living according to the general rules and "styles" approved by upper middle class Americans. (Or, alternatively, if you consider yourself a hippie, this would mean living according to what hippies say is right.)

3. *Live by expediency, not by rules.* This means doing what will achieve your ends in each individual situation. It usually means doing what somebody or some organization wants you to do, when that somebody or that organization (for example, your boss or a teacher) can either reward or punish you. It means pretty much ignoring the rules, unless the rule happens to be "expedient." It very much means "knowing which side your bread is buttered on."

4. *Live for others only,* which involves acting first and foremost to look out for the other fellow's welfare, and forgetting about your own welfare.

5. *Get so you truly understand and believe what Christianity is really all about, and then live according to your beliefs as a Christian*—something that involves, partially, "living for others," but also involves a lot more—a very "special" way of believing.

Section C—One Session (50 minutes):

OBJECTIVE: *To enable the group to explore any disparities there may be between their preferred life style and their priority life goals.*

Before the session begins, prepare a chart for *each* life goal by doing the following:

—Multiply the vote values given to each life-style option by the previously calculated "average priority ranking" given to that life goal. Doing this gives a different value to the various life styles; that is, it "weights" them according to the significance of the actual life goal.

EXAMPLE:

Life styles	Life goal: Achievement*		
	Vote values	*X priority ranking**	*Weighted value*
Self	63	X 4	252
Group	58	X 4	232
Expediency	69	X 4	276
Others	40	X 4	160
Christianity	25	X 4	100

*We gave "Achievement" a hypothetical average priority value of 4. In an actual group, the ranking might be different.

—Now add up the weighted values of each life style to get a total weighted value for that particular life style: in this example, 1,020. The totals of the five weighted values on all twelve charts are likely to be in the 1,000's. What will really affect their relative overall value, however, will be the "multiplier"—i.e., the priority rankings used to multiply or weight the original vote values. If "Achievement" had had an average priority value of 6 instead of 4, the total weighted value would have been 1,530.

SESSION:

Using a chart that records the grand-total scores for each life style, explain to the group how you derived the scores shown.

1. Analyzing one life goal at a time, you multiplied the vote values they gave in comparing life styles by the average priority ranking they originally gave to each life goal—thus coming up with a weighted score.

2. The weighted score reflects not only the relative "efficiency" of each life style, but also its relative importance in terms of coming out with certain desired results. If necessary, to get the point across, show an example of how this was done.

3. Show how a given life style might have come out with a very different score had you multiplied its total vote values by a different priority ranking.

4. Discuss the following:

   (a) Does your actual life tend to reflect the "life-style values" shown? If yes, how? If no, why not?

   (b) Are you unwittingly acting out a life style that is in conflict with your real life goals? If so, how? Or are your real life goals—not the ones you give lip service to, but the ones you act on—reflected by the ways in which you live?

   (c) Which do you think is the better way to approach life? To start living a "different style" or to give conscious thought to your real life goals and priorities? Or, can you do both?

Cultural Values
and
Morality

THREE TO FOUR SESSIONS: (45 minutes each.)

OBJECTIVE: *To increase the group's understanding that many decisions in life force people to choose between conflicting loyalties.*

Session One

1. Distribute copies of the sheet headed MILITARY COURT-MARTIAL (page 44), and have someone read it aloud while the others follow.

2. Explain that the group will hold the trial with
—one-third as a team of defense attorneys
—one-third as a team of prosecuting attorneys
—one-third as a team of judges

The judges will decide whether the defendant is guilty or not guilty and, if guilty, they will hand down a sentence from the possible alternatives. The judges will decide by majority vote; therefore, there must be an uneven number of judges.

Explain that you will serve as an officer of the court explaining the rules of the court.

3. Have the group divide into the three teams. Explain that they are under no circumstances to discuss the case with one another before the trial. Have the teams work in separate locations so that they cannot overhear each other.

4. Explain that in the next session you will hold the court-martial. The following will take place in the trial.
—The prosecuting attorney team will have 5 minutes to state their opening arguments to the court.
—Following this, the defense attorney team will have 5 minutes to state their opening arguments.
—No interruptions will be allowed during these opening arguments, and this restriction includes the judges.
—Afterward, the judges will spend the balance of the session cross-examining each team of attorneys to get at any further information they need.

5. After the teams have separated, give each person a copy of the appropriate material: DEFENSE ATTORNEYS, PROSECUTING ATTORNEYS, JUDGES (pages 45-47).

6. Have the two teams of attorneys plan their opening arguments. Have the judges become thoroughly familiar with their task. At the end again be sure each team knows they are not to discuss any aspect of the case with anyone not on their team.

Session Two:

1. Have the room set up as a courtroom with the judges at a head table and the two teams of attorneys at separate tables.

2. Post on newsprint the procedure for this session as outlined in session one and go over it with the group. In addition, explain that as an officer of the court you will see that the proceedings stay within the boundaries of judicial procedure, that is, *all* arguments made to the judges; no arguments between attorneys; no hearsay evidence admitted.

Session Three and (if needed) Session Four:

1. Have all participants resume their seats.

2. Let both teams of attorneys make any "closing arguments"—for no more than 5 minutes each.

3. Have each judge cast a written ballot of "Guilty" or "Not guilty" (but not the sentence).

4. Collect these ballots, and announce the results.

5. Continue to have the judges cast ballots until a majority is reached. The judges may talk briefly among themselves between ballots.

6. If a verdict of guilty is reached, do the same thing to get a majority opinion on sentencing.

For the remainder of Session Three, and in a fourth session if it is necessary, discuss:

1. What was the real problem in this case?

2. What tactics did the prosecuting attorneys use? How did you respond to those tactics?

3. What did the defense attorneys need to do to win the case?

4. In your opinion, who had the most difficult job in the case? Why?

5. How does what the Church teaches enter into situations like this?

6. Do you think you have to or will have to face decisions like this? How?

The case is the court-martial of a naval officer, the captain of a destroyer. He is accused of misbehavior before the enemy.

In that, Captain —————, being in the presence of the enemy, did, on the U.S.S. —————, on or about —————, 19—, by wilfully failing to pursue the enemy, failed to do his utmost to engage the enemy as it was his duty to do.

Charge: Violation of Uniform Code of Military Justice, Article 99.

The penalties permissible under the Code are as follows:

1. If the defendant is flagrantly guilty of failing to pursue and attack the enemy for reasons of cowardice or treason, then the possible penalties are:

    A. Death by military execution.

    B. Confinement at hard labor for life, with dishonorable discharge, denial of all pay, and dismissal from the naval service.

2. If the defendant failed to pursue and attack the enemy because of temporary emotional or psychological stress (temporary insanity) which can be proven to be severe enough to justify his actions, then the maximum penalty is:

    Confinement at hard labor for 10 years, forfeiture of all pay and allowances, and dismissal from the naval service.

3. If the defendant is found not guilty, then no sentence can be executed.

JUDGES TEAM

YOU ARE A TEAM OF JUDGES at a military tribunal. The case you are hearing is the court-martial of a naval officer, the captain of a destroyer. He is accused of misbehavior before the enemy.

Until the court-martial begins, you know nothing more than this about the case. As judges at the court, your specific instructions are to determine the extent of guilt, if any, and to execute sentence according to the Uniform Code of Military Justice.

1. Determine whether or not the defendant is in fact guilty of the charge as stated; that is, whether or not he did in fact "fail to pursue and attack the enemy."

2. Even if the defendant is guilty of the actions stated, determine whether or not there is justification for sentencing him.

3. You must base your sentence and verdict on majority vote. To impose sentence of death, sentence must be unanimous. *First,* you must decide by majority whether or not guilt exists. If you decide the defendant is guilty, then, *second,* you must decide on a sentence. Your verdict is final.

4. Make sure that you understand the facts the attorneys present, and that you understand what a judge is supposed to do: objectively weigh the evidence and come to a just decision. It is impossible to decide on a given degree of guilt, and then not execute the sentence. Whatever degree of guilt you determine, you must choose from the available sentences for that degree of guilt.

YOU ARE A TEAM OF PROSECUTING ATTORNEYS at a military tribunal court-martial. The defendant you are prosecuting is a navy captain accused of dereliction of duty. These are the facts in the case:
  —It is wartime.
  —An enemy submarine sank a friendly troop transport.
  —The destroyer captain witnessed the sinking and rushed to the scene.
  —Upon arriving at the scene, the captain's sonarman indicated positive identification of a submarine lurking in the waters directly beneath the destroyer.
  —The captain gave orders to pick up the hundred or so survivors of the transport who were floating in the water around his ship.
  —The captain also gave specific orders not to do any depth charging.
  —Two hours later, twelve nautical miles away, a second troopship was sunk, presumably by the same submarine.
  —The Uniform Code of Military Justice specifically states that an officer's first and primary duty is to "pursue and attack the enemy at all costs." The captain's failure to do this is the reason why he is being prosecuted.

YOUR JOB IS AS FOLLOWS:

1. As prosecuting attorneys, your objective is to win a verdict of guilty, and to convince the court that the defendant is guilty for the most serious reasons possible. In other words, you are seeking the maximum penalty.

2. In their order of severity, here are the possible types of guilt in this case.
  —Cowardice or treason
  —Temporary insanity
  —Not guilty

3. As professional attorneys, your job is to make absolutely certain that the court makes its decision on legal grounds—on the law as it is written. The law in this case states very specifically that failing to pursue and attack the enemy is a crime under the circumstances.

4. Also, as professional attorneys you should seek the maximum penalty possible. In this case, if you can prove that the defendant did what he did because of cowardice or treason, you will have done your job in the most effective manner.

HERE ARE SOME FURTHER FACTS ABOUT THE DEFENDANT:

—He is forty-three years old and has been a naval officer for twenty years.
—He has been married and divorced. There were no children.
—A Chief Petty Officer from his ship told you during the pretrial investigation that "The old man (the defendant) had been kind of moody before the incident. He was really kind of trying to avoid action, if you ask me."
—The officer claims no religion and has his Executive Officer conduct the ship's religious services.
—He has a good record as an officer, save for this instance, and one other that occurred ten years ago. At that time, he was accused of striking a sailor on the head, in a moment of anger. He was found guilty and reprimanded, but not sentenced.

ONCE AGAIN, YOUR JOB IS TO

Plan all of the arguments you can think of to prove the defendant guilty for the most serious reasons that seem possible in the case.

DEFENSE ATTORNEYS TEAM

YOU ARE A TEAM OF DEFENSE ATTORNEYS in a military court-martial. Your job is to defend a naval officer accused of dereliction of duty. The facts of the case are as follows:

—It is wartime.
—An enemy submarine sank a friendly troop-ship.
—The destroyer captain witnessed the sinking and rushed to the scene.
—Upon arriving at the scene, the captain's sonarman indicated positive identification of a submarine lurking in the waters directly beneath the destroyer.
—The captain gave orders to pick up the hundred or so survivors of the transport who who were floating in the water around his ship.
—The captain also gave specific orders not to do any depth charging.
—Two hours later, twelve nautical miles away, a second troopship was sunk, presumably by the same submarine.
—The Uniform Code of Military Justice specifically states that an officer's first and primary duty is to "pursue and attack the enemy at all costs." The captain's failure to do this is the reason why he is being prosecuted.

YOUR JOB IS AS FOLLOWS:

1. As defense attorneys, your objective is, if possible, to win a verdict of "not guilty"—to show that your defendant did not do what he is charged with doing. If you cannot do this, then your objective is to show that your defendant had the best possible excuse for doing what he did.

2. Here are the possible verdicts that can be given by the court:
   —Not guilty is the best of all, for your defendant.
   —Guilty by reason of temporary insanity is the next best verdict.

—Guilty by reason of cowardice or treason is the worst verdict of all.

3. As professional attorneys, your job is to cast every doubt possible on what the prosecuting attorneys say. They must prove your client guilty beyond any reasonable doubt; therefore, anything you can do or say that will cast doubt will be useful. Any sort of argument, logical or illogical, if it will do this job of doubt-creating, is a good one to use.

HERE ARE SOME FURTHER FACTS ABOUT YOUR CLIENT:

—He is forty-three years old, and has been a naval officer for twenty years.
—His executive officer told you, during the pretrial examination: "The old man (the defendant) is a good officer. He's tough, but fair. He's always done his job to the best of his ability."

YOUR CLIENT TOLD YOU THE FOLLOWING:

"Look, being a naval officer is my career. But I'm also a human being. Have you ever seen what happens when you drop a depth charge in the water? It's incredible, the power of those things.

"If I'd started dropping depth charges all over the place, I'd have killed every one of those people in the water. They were hurt and crying for help. How could I just ignore them? Even worse, how could I look at myself afterward if I'd killed them?

"We never actually saw the sub. We got a positive sonar report, but how do I know that was really a submarine below us? It could have been a whale or something else!"

SPECIAL NOTE: In planning your arguments do not rely too much on solely "moral" arguments. Try to fight the case issue by issue, trying first to cast doubt on the whole question of any guilt ("he didn't really do it"), then fighting out each possible reason for guilt. Hold the "moral" argument as a last reserve.

THREE SESSIONS: (45 minutes each.)

OBJECTIVE: *To enlarge the group's awareness of the historic and present realities of:*
  (a) *ways in which worldly political power may be exercised;*
  (b) *how "religion" may be viewed by persons with political power.*

INTRODUCTION: These three sessions are based on a series of hypothetical memorandums between Pontius Pilate and his boss, the "Chief of Overseas Operations," located in Rome.

Because the material in the memos focuses on the events surrounding Jesus' death and resurrection, you might want to use them in the weeks preceding Easter or for a weekend conference at that time of year.

Session One:

1. Distribute copies of MEMOS 1A and 1B (pages 49-50). Have the group read them through.
  2. Discuss 1A. Ask:
    (a) "How would you describe Pilate?"
    (b) "How is he trying to appear to his boss?"
    (c) "What is Pilate most concerned about in his job?"
    (d) "Are there politicians like Pilate today? Who? How do they act?"
  3. Discuss 1B. Ask:
    (a) "How would you describe the 'Chief'?"
    (b) "How does the chief treat Pilate?"
    (c) "What does the chief think is important for Pilate to do?"
    (d) "Are there people like the chief today? Who? How do they act?"
    (e) "Are there people today who act as the chief says—keeping their nose to the grindstone to make a buck and using spectator sports or other entertainment to blow off steam?"
    (f) "So-called 'idealists' are, in the chief's eyes, a good deal more dangerous to society than merely violent types. Is anybody talking (or thinking) that way nowadays? Who are our 'dreamers'? Who is violent?"

Session Two:

1. Distribute copies of MEMOS 2A and 2B (pages 51-52), and have the group read them.
  2. Discuss 2A. Ask:
    (a) "How would you describe Pilate now?"
    (b) "How has he responded to the advice from his boss?"
    (c) "Are there people today who react in any of the ways Pilate did—
      —"Surprised that a 'gentle, scholarly type' can be violent?
      —"Offended by those not as 'clean' as themselves?
      "Engaged in petty graft?"
  Ask for examples of such people.
  3. Discuss 2B. Ask:
    (a) "What is the chief worried about? Are there people like him today? Who? How do they act?"
    (b) "What does the chief think Pilate ought to do? Anybody advocating quick, heavy crackdowns today? Who? Where?"
    (c) "How does the chief see religion in relation to politics? Do you know people with similar views? Who? Why do you think they believe as they do?"

Session Three:

1. Distribute MEMOS 3A and 3B (pages 53-55). Have the group read them.
  2. Discuss 3A. Ask:
    "What's with Pilate now? What has happened to him? How would you describe his reactions?"
  3. Discuss 3B. Ask:
    (a) "How does the chief treat Pilate?"
    (b) "What is the chief's view of 'duty' versus people? Does anybody today believe and act that way? Who? How?"
    (c) "What good advice does the chief give Pilate as a cure for his upsetness? What do you think of his advice? Do you know others who look at life and religion that way?"

MEMO 1A

Memo To: *Chief of Overseas Operations*
  From: *P. Pilate*

Well, Boss, things seem to be humming along fairly well out here. I trust you noticed in my report that collections were up again. Not an easy job, either, in a place as poor as this.

Frankly, it would be a lot less poor if these people spent more time working and less time arguing. They will literally talk your head off about anything. They're as bad as the Greeks that way.

Herod is being his usual obnoxious self. Still, he's not too hard to keep in line, if you just remember to flatter his ego. You'll be glad to hear most people have pretty much forgotten that cute stunt he pulled a year or two back. I told him then, well, that would just be *it* for him. I guess you have to be a local to appreciate the humor in putting a head on a platter. Anyway, I don't think Salome is *that* cute.

Things are as calm as you can expect in a place like this. Oh, we have the usual number of nuts running around the countryside spouting off about this or that. But I don't get overly concerned about them. It must be an occupational disease around here—the heat, or something—that turns these characters on. Fortunately, these itinerant lecturers spend most of their time berating their own people, not us.

Right now, for instance, there's an ex-carpenter (get that) who is drawing pretty fair crowds out in the sticks. It beats me why the local big-wigs at the temple get so upset about him, though. As far as I can tell, he's just telling people they ought to shape up, but to hear the chief priest tell it, he's an out-and-out traitor.

Well, I better drop this, and start organizing. There's a big holiday brewing here—the Jews call it the Passover. It has to do with their religion, and it always draws a big crowd to the city, with the usual share of troublemakers. I'm figuring on full security measures. The first firebrand who tries to organize a demonstration is, believe me, going to have his head cracked open with a nightstick.

Cordially,

Pilate

Memo To: *P. Pilate, Jerusalem*
  From: *The Chief*

Your note encourages me, for the most part. Keep up the good work.

I quite realize that your job is no bed of roses. Please bear in mind, though, that governorships are hard to come by. If you just stay with it, though, I guarantee that I'll put you at the top of the list for the next good slot. Who knows, sunny Sicily, or perhaps the south of France? Maybe even a position here at headquarters.

Now, I must caution you on one point, and I hope you'll understand that I'm not trying to be overcritical. Really, you have a tendency at times, though, to be a bit flippant about serious matters. I already know that your Herod is a double-crossing, ill-mannered old coot if there ever was one. But do not regard him too lightly. He can be a most valuable ally, especially in times of trouble.

If nothing else, he both can and will put down any trouble, using ways and means you might never imagine. That's one of the keys you must remember. There are things you can never do because you have a reputation to protect (and anyhow, you would be too squeamish). That's why having a nasty friend sometimes proves helpful. Certainly, in the foreign service you can use all the friends you can get. So keep working on Herod, even if he's not the type of person you'd have for cocktails.

I have noticed you frequently mention these itinerant preachers and teachers running around Palestine. Again, I think you may be underestimating a possibly serious situation.

Bear in mind, Pontius, that the most valuable subject people are those most resembling our own native Romans, or at least the more clearheaded northern types. That is, we need people who are sober, hardworking, no-nonsense types; people who know the value of a dollar; people who use up their energy in productive work. Secondly, and this may sound a bit silly at first, we need people who are easy to entertain.

Let me be quite clear about this, though it may sound somewhat overphilosophical to you. Take first a man whose whole energies are devoted to winning his daily bread. Now, that is a very "safe" man. He has little time for idle dreaming, and no energy for mischief. Surely that makes sense to you, doesn't it?

Second, my point about recreation. As you know, all of us are heirs to a certain amount of frustration. From time to time everybody needs to blow off a little steam. And that, my friend, is why a steady round of fairly exciting recreation—things like gladiatorial sports, and the more serious brand of entertainment—are most important in your administration.

I don't mean to sound preachy, but it troubles me that you haven't considered these matters more seriously. You see, the way I read your situation, you have a rather large percentage of your people who are what I would call "dreamers." More than that, those Jews seem predisposed to all sorts of idealistic gas. What you interpret as a mere tendency toward argumentation—harmless, though noisy—could become a source of real trouble.

Believe me, I have seen where it can lead!! I well remember the situation I faced in Greece. Before we got wise to them (we had always figured that Greeks just liked to talk a lot) we found ourselves facing riots, and strikes, and no end of trouble. It cost us plenty to get the Greeks back in line, and we would have been spared that trouble and bloodshed if we had only recognized the simple fact that talk eventually leads to action. Give me those simple-minded barbarians any time. They run around in the woods beating up one another, but they don't think very much. They are a *lot* less dangerous.

Well, enough of this. I trust by the time this arrives you'll be well organized to handle the "mob." The weather is getting quite warm here in Rome. Am thinking about a vacation in Spain, unless somebody dreams up a really exotic new colosseum show. (If I see one more lion and tiger fight I think I shall go mad.)

My best to you and yours.

Sincerely,

The Chief

Memo To: *The Chief*
    From: *P. Pilate*

Thanks for your thoughtful note. I didn't mean to sound "flippant," as you put it. No one knows better than I what can happen when people get filled up with their own ideals.

I also buy your notion about that reprobate, Herod. He has a pretty bloody track record, but he knows what he's doing, and he doesn't forget which side his bread is buttered on. Talked to him just the other day, as a matter of fact. Turns out he's about as much in the dark as I am about what makes these people tick. (He's not Jewish, you know.) We pretty much agree that these hare-brained types aren't quite as bad as you think, however.

You see, people are poor around here. The way we see it, if their own leaders can keep them concerned about things like personal ethics—and especially if they worry about some kind of afterlife, versus life— why, that can't be bad, can it?

Matter of fact, that carpenter I was telling you about—the fellow from Nazareth, some godforsaken town south of here—is a pretty good case in point. My field representatives tell me he's talking up the *virtues* of poverty!

Now that I think of it, though, even he gave me some cause for concern this week. Seems he arrived at the start of the holiday week, and some of the townsfolk gave him a big reception. Nothing wrong with that, but one of the local priests came running in unannounced, mad as a boiled owl. It seems this guy's reception went to his head, or something. Everybody had been calling him their "savior," and then next thing you know he marches on the temple. Believe it or not, he went in with a whip and started beating up the local merchants. Trouble, with a capital "T."

Listen, those guys who change money at the temple are as crooked as a used-chariot salesman, but I can't have somebody tearing up things this way. Anyhow, he got away, and hasn't been seen for the last few days. But, like you said, even the idealists can make trouble if you're not careful.

By the way, Herod tipped me off that the religion politicos are planning some sort of legal action against the fellow. Crazy, isn't it?

I wish I could go to the south of anywhere. There must be a million or more people jammed in this city—mostly unwashed. I think I'm going to institute a new ruling: baths and haircuts for everybody! A bad idea, perhaps, but you should smell them.

Anyway, I'll sure be glad when this week is over. The troops are skittish, the priests are mad, Herod (as usual) is drunk, and I'm tired. But, we should make a pretty good pile on our cut of the temple profits. Like you say, it pays to have a friend in the right places.

Cordially,

Pilate

Memo To: *P. Pilate*
  From: *The Chief*

I trust next time you'll heed my advice!

I don't mean to say "I told you so," but now you've seen it for yourself. That business with the temple is typical. Businessmen are almost always the first ones to be attacked by people who have an ax to grind. Frankly, it doesn't even make that much difference whether they're shady dealers or not.

I tell you that this is an object lesson. This wouldn't have occurred in the first place if you had those people in line the way I told you. You give these world-changers their head, and they turn from mild dreamers into monsters.

This carpenter is a perfect case in point. Sure, you may think he's just one more tub-thumper for a worthy cause. In a sense, you're right. But he upsets people. It all starts with bull sessions, but then people get stirred up. They start thinking. Next thing you know, you have riots in the streets.

You may not have seen the last of this, either, my friend. Trouble comes in bunches, and now that one guy has gotten away with a swipe at the establishment, a lot more are going to think they can do it, too. Take my advice, if there's some way to put this carpenter on ice, do it in a hurry. Extralegally, if necessary.

Do you think those people might be interested in colosseum games? I saw the most amazing act, involving Numidians, Gauls, and some elephants. It takes your breath away!

Oh, one more thing. Claudius has been locked up with his astrologers most of this month. If you quote me on this, I'll have your head, but I think the old man's turning into some kind of religious nut! He has those quacks staring into the entrails of owls—disgusting—and then he decides what to do. Whatever happened to good old-fashioned practical politicians?

My best to your wife—and please, try to keep the lid on. A few judiciously cracked skulls right now might be just the medicine for putting those people back on the right track.

Sincerely,

The Chief

Memo To: *The Chief*
   From: *P. Pilate*

Bad news and good, I'm afraid. I'll start with the bad.

In the first place, this has to have been one of the craziest, mixed-up weeks of my career. I most ruefully admit, once again, you knew what you were talking about. Especially about that damnable carpenter! The fellow—name of Jesus, by the way—stirred up a real hornet's nest.

Looking back on it, I should have stepped in a whole lot earlier. But I thought if I just stayed clear of the whole mess, it would go away.

In the first place, that villainous crew of priests at the temple played me for a sucker. They meant business about doing this fellow Jesus in. They worked a deal to arrest him, on some weird combination of treason and heresy. (Heresy, I realize, is hardly a capital offense with us, but these people take their religion pretty seriously. They were figuring to execute him.)

Apparently, these Jews have been looking a long time for a savior to arrive—a "Messiah" they call him—and this Jesus claimed to be it. And that is either the thing that set off the local priests, or else they used it as an excuse. With these Palestinians you can never quite untangle what they say and what they mean.

At first, I figured "So what?" As far as I'm concerned, you can claim to be Zeus, or Caesar himself, for all I care, if you mind your own business. But these crazy people were fixing to string the poor guy up for what he was saying. (Incidentally, now that I think about it, what probably really upset some of the bigwigs was the fact they thought Jesus would cut into the temple profits. That I can understand, at least.)

Still and all, it wouldn't have turned out badly, except, like I say, they fooled me. They concocted a phony trial, to make it look legal—and they tried to play off the sentencing, first on Herod, and then on me.

Herod is no dummy. He wouldn't touch this one with a fork, so you know who got stuck with the can of worms.

They brought the fellow to me. A pretty bedraggled sight, frankly. But—and this is one of the things that upsets me—he turned out, really, to be an awfully nice guy. Mixed up, maybe, but hardly a criminal. He didn't say much—and, yes, he mentioned something about being a king, but "not of this world"—but everything about him said loud and clear, "Here is a good man."

Oh, I know that sounds maudlin. But I can count on the fingers of one hand the number of good men I've ever known. Take it from me, this was one of those. Far as I could tell, he was sorrier for me than I was for him.

I'm rambling. I dropped the case and gave him back to the loving hands of the priests. They promptly rigged up another deal, where I had to let a real crook out of jail (I'll tell you how that works some other time) and substitute this Jesus for him.

Well, there isn't much more to this part of the story. I hear some of the troops roughed the guy up pretty badly, and then, last Friday, they crucified him along with a couple of ordinary burglars.

Now look, what follows is going to make me sound a little peculiar. I won't say flat-out what I do and don't believe, but I'd be interested in your reaction—and advice.

—First, my wife starts having these crazy dreams. Says I shouldn't have had anything to do with the carpenter. She seems horrified by him, and by the whole situation.

—Point two, the carpenter died the very day they nailed him up. Most people take longer, so that made me wonder a little. He didn't look that frail.

—Point three, we had a storm-and-a-half last Friday—just, it would appear, as the man died—complete with earth tremors. Apparently a veil of some sort in the temple was split in two, and this was predicted and is somehow supposed to be connected to this crucified man.

—Point four (if you're still with me), the man had specifically told his friends that (a) he would be killed; (b) after three days he would come to life again; and (c) that this was the proof he was what he said he was—a god, or son of god, or from god, or something.

—Point five—it's now Tuesday, five days after the execution—and I'm getting rumors from unimpeachable sources that he *did* come to life again. I even checked his burial spot, and sure enough, there's nothing there. (Maybe that doesn't mean much—but on the other hand there were two trusted and hardboiled guards stationed there. What happened?) Another thing: I've heard of people claiming they would come back to life. And I've heard tales of it being true. But from everything I can gather, this guy *did*. Either that, or I am surrounded by fools, liars, or both. For instance, the people who are making this claim are really running a colossal risk even talking about this Jesus any more. They could be killed next. And what did happen to him, anyway? Are all these people crazy, or don't they care if they die?

Am I losing my mind, chief? If this thing is true, something *very* strange happened. (Not only that, I now discover this same fellow is responsible for bringing somebody *else* back to life earlier in the year.) If it's not true, then people have started acting differently than I ever saw them act in all my life.

In any case, the rumor is spreading much too fast for my comfort. Now what do I do? I mean, I'm not too happy about letting this man get killed in the first place. What if he's up and about again? And what do I do to stop this rumor?

Now for the good news: We made a record haul over the week. If I can just keep that greedy Herod from siphoning off too much of it, the revenue picture should be excellent. I just wish, chief, I felt better about this whole thing.

Regretfully,

Pilate

MEMO 3B

Memo To: *P. Pilate*
From: *The Chief*

My dear fellow! How you do run on about trifles. Let me sum up my thoughts concerning your recent affair:

1. You seem to be making mountains out of mole-hills. When one considers the tide of world events from my perspective, one realizes that the life or death of an unknown carpenter in the far reaches of the civilized world makes scarcely any difference one way or the other.

2. You have obviously let your emotions get in the way of your good sense. Nobody claims the decisions a provincial governor must make are always easy. But can't you see that, in actuality, you only did what had to be done? In my opinion, you deserve not criticism but praise for exhibiting rare good sense. From what you have told me, making no decision about this Jesus' fate was the best decision. So you were tricked a bit—that is not the worst that could have happened.

3. Since it is not our policy to exercise "thought control," you need not become so concerned over what these provincials believe. The fact that rumors are spreading about a man coming back to life simply reflects the original belief that this man was a god, or from god. I will predict the outcome. Since these people are so embroiled with religion, it will not be long before new, and perhaps even wilder ideas attract their loyalty. They will forget this Jesus. So long as you yourself stay on an even keel, it cannot possibly make that much difference what a group of religious fanatics believes.

4. To reiterate: this rumor will die away and be replaced by others. That is the one fortunate thing about the hodge-podge of religious beliefs in the world. With all of them shouting they are right, they tend to cancel one another out. Also to reiterate: the job of a politician is above religious fanaticism.

5. As to your particular feelings, and those of your wife, learn to take things in stride, old fellow. You are simply going through the pangs of power. When you are in a position to wield power, you must at times make decisions that dissatisfy people—sometimes even yourself!

But duty first. You have, among other things, the duty of repressing your so-called "humane instincts" at times, in order to do what is most practical. Practicality, above all things, is a necessity in your work. That is the way of the world. As I say, if you could view the event from a loftier point of view, you would see that the possible unfairness to one man (however just he might be) must be balanced against the overall good. I know that sounds hard, even cruel. But first things first. In this case, there was really little else you could do, don't you agree?

I believe, Pontius, you should plan a brief vacation from your duties. Perhaps a pleasant cruise on the Mediterranean—delightful this time of year, I am told.

The break will do you no end of good. When you arrive back in Palestine, you will surely find yourself full of the old vim and vigor. This little affair has taxed you far too greatly, largely because you have been overworked of late. Had you been in better shape, I am sure you would have done just what you did—but without the emotional hangovers.

To more pleasant subjects, the state of the Empire at large seems excellent. We are even enjoying reasonable calm on the northern borders these days. I should think that before long you can look forward to a cushy position in some more attractive location. Alexandria may be opening soon, and there are even some choice positions soon to be vacated right here in Rome.

Enjoy your vacation, and forget everything about this man Jesus, and all those other noisy Jews. The world holds better things, and you are better off trying to shove the whole thing aside. As a good friend once told me, "accentuate the positive."

Sincerely,

The Chief

FOUR SESSIONS: (45 minutes each.)

OBJECTIVE: *To enable the group to explore in depth:*
  (a) *How the self-interest and other values of individuals affect their actions;*
  (b) *The issue of civil disobedience;*
  (c) *What young people can do about injustices in society.*

Session One:

1. Explain to the group that they will be conducting the trial of a teenager involved in vandalism.

2. Give everyone a copy of the sheet headed TRIAL OF ARTHUR WOODS (page 58), and have someone read it aloud with the others following.

3. Distribute copies of ARTHUR WOODS' STATEMENT TO HIS ATTORNEYS (page 64). Have someone read it aloud with the others following.

4. Explain that the group will be divided into
  —Defense Counsel Team
  —Prosecuting Attorney Team
  —Three witnesses—Plant Guard, Police Officer, Flameout Chemical Company Officer

Arthur Woods is not included since he will not testify. Explain that you will be the judge.

5. Make the decisions about who will take each role. If the group is larger than twelve, create additional roles: a member of the plant guard's family, or another guard; another officer or two of the Flameout company; other police officers or members of the police officer's family. These extra characters could meet with the witness and help him or her get into the role. During the trial they could be present in the courtroom. Explain that the group will have the remainder of the session to prepare for the trial using material you have for each role. The trial will be held in the next session.

6. Distribute the material provided for each role and spend the rest of the time moving from group to group assisting as needed with preparations for the trial.

Session Two:

1. Arrange the room as a courtroom—judge at a head table; defense counsel and prosecuting attorneys at separate tables facing the judge; witnesses seated behind the attorneys. If there are persons assigned the roles of family, friends, or others connected with the witnesses, they should sit with their witness in the courtroom.

2. Explain that following the trial—which may continue for another session—the entire group will vote for a verdict. A majority vote will determine the verdict. (Have possible verdicts posted on the wall on newsprint.)

3. Conduct the trial. Divide whatever time you have so that the prosecution and defense have equal time.

A witness is called and examined by one of the prosecuting attorneys. Then one of the defense attorneys conducts a cross-examination. As the judge, adhere to the rules of evidence as much as possible.

4. Explain what the first step in the next session will be.

Session Three:

1. Conclude the formal trial using the courtroom setting. Have each team of attorneys make their closing arguments for 5 minutes. First, the prosecution speaks; then the defense.

2. As the judge, explain that you now want an informal discussion of the pros and cons to help you reach a decision. Have the attorneys discuss with you with the others listening. The attorneys are still trying to "win," but in the informal discussion various extenuating circumstances can be brought out which were not permissible in the court.

3. When it seems appropriate, begin voting by written ballot for a verdict. Everyone has one vote. Refer to the possible verdicts on newsprint. Either *Guilty*—of which charges and with what extenuating circumstances, if any —or *Not guilty*.

4. Read the ballots and list totals on newsprint. If there is no majority, then repeat the voting. If possible reach a majority opinion at least of guilty or not guilty; and if guilty, of which charges.

Session Four:

Discuss the ramifications of the trial in three areas:

A. How the self-interest and other values of individuals affected their actions—
  Discuss the plant guard—
      the police officer—
      the company officer—
      Arthur Woods—
For each one ask:
  (a) "What was he personally most concerned about?"
  (b) "What are your feelings and reactions toward him?"

B. The issue of civil disobedience—Ask: "Do you feel that civil disobedience is ever justified? If so, when? How? If not, why not?"

C. The issue of what young people can do about injustices in society. Read aloud the part of Arthur Wood's statement beginning, "So that's what happened . . ." to the end.

Ask: "Do you think Arthur is right in feeling helpless as a young person in dealing effectively with problems in our society? If so, why? If not, why not?"

These are the facts:

1. On the night of October 17 a number of persons broke into the corporate office of the Flameout Chemical Company. According to the police report, a total of fifteen young people entered the building at about 9 p.m. There were eight boys and seven girls.

2. The group broke in through a first-floor window. They proceeded to ransack various files, upset desks and empty their contents, and smear obscene words on the walls, using paint and brushes which they brought with them.

3. A plant guard who tried to stop the vandalism was struck down by one of the boys. His jaw was broken and, as a result, he missed two weeks of work. No one is sure who struck the guard.

4. Other guards in the plant called the police, who arrived on the scene at 9:30 p.m. and arrested the entire group of young people.

5. One policeman was bitten on the hand by a girl. A second policeman was struck in the face by a boy —not the defendant named above, however.

6. Marijuana was discovered in the purse of one of the girls.

Since the night of the arrest, the defendants have been free on bail. All are to be tried as a group except for the defendant, Arthur Woods, who is to be tried individually. His family has employed the most highly paid lawyer in town to defend him.

The possible verdicts in the case:

1. Guilty of breaking and entering, vandalism, assault and battery, and resisting arrest.

2. Guilty of one or more of these four charges, but not all four.

3. Guilty of one or more of the charges, but with various extenuating circumstances (such as resisting arrest due to excessive police force).

4. Not guilty.

PROSECUTING ATTORNEY TEAM

Your team plays the part of the prosecuting attorney in a trial involving a seventeen-year-old high school student named Arthur Woods.

What You Are to Do

Your job is to argue your case before the judge in such a way that you achieve the maximum possible verdict. The possible verdicts include:

1. Guilty of breaking and entering, vandalism, assault and battery, and resisting arrest.
2. Guilty of one or more of these four charges, but not all four.
3. Guilty of one or more of the charges, but with various extenuating circumstances (such as resisting arrest due to excessive police force).
4. Not guilty.

In planning your strategy, remember that it is up to you to prove beyond a reasonable doubt that the defendant did in fact commit each crime of which he is charged, beginning with proof that the defendant was in fact present and did in fact know what he was doing.

You know that the defense attorney will not permit his client to testify. As a result, you plan to call three witnesses to the stand. These include:

a. The plant guard, to help establish the presence of the defendant at the scene and shed light on the assault and battery aspects of the case.
b. The police officer who physically apprehended this particular defendant.
c. The treasurer of the company, to testify as to actual damage that occurred. The treasurer also saw all of the defendants at the jail, the night they were arrested.

Your team represents the defense counsel for one Arthur Woods, a seventeen-year-old high school student, accused of breaking and entering, vandalism, assault and battery, and resisting arrest.

You command the highest fees in the city, and this student's parents are very wealthy. Arthur's father owns a drug company.

Since the night of the arrest, the defendants have been free on bail. All are to be tried as a group except for your client who, because of your efforts, is to be tried individually.

One of the first things you did was ask your client to tell you his version of what occurred, and why he was involved. You have a transcript of his statement.

What You Are to Do

Because your client is a minor, his trial will be held before a judge, without a jury being involved. Your job is, if possible, to win a verdict of not guilty. Otherwise, your job is to achieve the least serious verdict for your client, with the least penalty involved.

The possible verdicts in this case are:

1. Guilty of *all* charges (breaking and entering plus vandalism, assault and battery, resisting arrest).
2. Guilty of fewer charges (breaking and entering plus vandalism, or vandalism and resisting arrest, etc., anything less than all four charges).
3. Guilty of one or more of the charges, but with extenuating circumstances. (For instance, resisting arrest because of excessive police force, or perhaps carrying out these acts without full knowledge of their gravity.)
4. Not guilty.

In planning your defense, remember that it is up to the state to prove beyond a reasonable doubt that:

—Your client actually was there.

—Your client actually broke and entered, actually participated in the vandalism, actually helped assault the guard, and actually resisted arrest.

—Your client knew what he was doing, and knew it was wrong.

In the trial, your client will not testify. The prosecution plans to call as its witnesses the plant guard, one of the arresting police officers, and an officer of the company.

PLANT GUARD

You are a night guard at the Flameout Chemical Company. About 9 o'clock on the evening of October 17, you heard a disturbance in one of the offices of the plant.

You went to these offices and heard a commotion inside. It sounded as though things were being tipped over and broken. You also heard several voices, both male and female. They sounded like young people.

You opened the door and saw a number of people with flashlights, moving about. You were struck on the side of the face. You never saw your assailant, since the force of the blow thrust you against the door jamb, and that, in turn, knocked you unconscious.

When you came to, you saw a group of about a dozen teenagers standing in the middle of the room, surrounded by helmeted police. They were all handcuffed, and you noticed a few of them were bruised and bleeding.

You stood by as the group was led outside.

The attorney general has informed you that one of this group is to be tried individually. (The others are being tried in a group.) He showed you a picture of this defendant, and you recognized him as one of the boys in the group you discovered.

You are being called as a witness in a trail of this defendant. The trial has been delayed so that you would be able to talk. Up to this time, your jaw has been wired shut as a result of the blow you received that night.

To help you play your role as the plant guard, consider how you have been insulted: You have sustained a personal injury; lost time; and suffered pain. You are trying to make a living, and these punk kids ought to be severely punished. On the other hand, you really don't know all that went on because you lost consciousness before you could clearly see what was happening.

You are a patrolman who is part of a special riot control squad. There are thirty members of this squad, and your particular job is controlling public disorders of any kind.

Last October 17 your squad was called into action because of a disturbance at the Flameout Chemical Company. Not knowing the size or nature of this disturbance, all thirty members went into action.

You arrived on the scene at about 9:30 p.m. When the site of the commotion was identified—a first-floor office at the rear of the building—your captain directed you and several other officers to go to that location. The balance of the squad was let in through the main door by plant guards.

When you arrived in the rear, you heard loud sounds coming out of a window as though furniture were being broken. The window was broken, and inside you could discern a group of people.

You went up to the window, and immediately came face-to-face with one boy—a teenager you would guess to be around seventeen or eighteen years old. On a prearranged signal, you entered through this window, as your fellow officers entered the room through the doors on the opposite side.

One youngster—you think it was probably the same boy you first saw—was standing just to your left as you got through the window. He raised his hands, and acting on the strength both of instinct and long training (as well as experience) you immediately struck him across both wrists. He ducked away, and you hit him across the back to put him on the floor.

He stated something like, "I quit," or words to that effect, and you told him not to move. (You don't recall your exact words, since at that moment you moved on to capture another individual.)

The only lights in the room were flashlights, their beams illuminating a melee of struggling bodies. First making sure the open window was still guarded, you plunged in. Although the whole affair got pretty hectic, you recall certain events. You grabbed hold of someone's sweatshirt, at the neck and from the rear, to throw the individual to the ground. It turned out to be a girl. Also, jabbing with your nightstick, you managed to subdue another youngster. At the time,

he was fighting with an officer, so you feel your action was highly justified. Later on, you found this same officer had been badly bitten on the thumb of his left hand by one of the girls.

Within a few minutes, your group had rounded up the intruders. There were eight boys and seven girls, all between the ages of fifteen and nineteen.

When the lights came on, you noticed obscene words painted on the walls and the fact that furniture and files had been upturned or emptied. One of the expressions on the walls was: "Down with war-mongers and pigs."

You are being called to testify against one of these young people. The others are to be tried in a group, but this individual—Arthur Woods—will be tried by himself.

Several thoughts arise in you at this time. You are an "honest cop." You try to do your duty. Your job is not easy, and it is often dangerous. You were in the Korean War and received several awards for bravery. Your income is quite modest, and it takes everything you have to make ends meet.

You do not like to be characterized as a "pig." You most certainly don't like to be characterized as brutal. If, at times, you have to use force, that is because there is no other way to do your job. As far as you can see, no amount of talking would have stopped these young people from doing what they did. You know that this defendant is one you saw in the window; the one you hit on the wrists and back. You suspect his attorney may try to charge police brutality. You have your answer ready: When a person in a violent situation raises his hands as if to strike, you don't give him a second chance. That might be your last chance.

To help you play your role as the police officer: You are honestly convinced you executed your duties in a proper manner. You have a somewhat defensive attitude—you are misrepresented by these young people; their attitudes conflict with your own beliefs; you believe firmly in the rights of private property, the essential need for the Vietnam war, and the need for your own job.

COMPANY OFFICER

You are the vice-president and treasurer of the Flameout Chemical Company.

On the night of October 17, fifteen teenagers broke into one of your company's offices and committed various acts of vandalism. Files were broken into, desks were overturned and scratched, papers were strewn around, and words—some of them obscene—painted on the walls.

Your comptroller has provided you with exact figures on the damage: It comes to a total of $8,900, although this figure does not account for the time that will be required to reassemble missing files.

There is another reason why this concerns you, however. For about eleven months, you have been negotiating with a large defense contractor to provide them with the raw materials needed in the manufacture of high-explosive shells. Basically, your firm would provide the powder used in forming the explosive elements of these shells.

This strikes you as slightly ironic, since you have become aware, through newspaper articles, that these young people invaded your offices because they thought your company manufactured napalm. That is not the case. So far, you have never manufactured war materials.

Your concern is that important, and highly confidential, materials may have been lost during the vandalism.

Now you are being called as a witness in the trial of one of the intruders: a seventeen-year-old boy named Arthur Woods. All the others are being tried in a group. This defendant is being tried individually.

On the night of the incident, after your president was informed, he called and directed you to go down to the jail and talk to the police. At that time, you also took a look at the defendants and talked to a few of them.

You saw Arthur Woods at the jail. You did not talk to Woods, however, and for a reason. He is the son of a man named Howard Woods. Howard Woods is the president of a company known as Woods Pharmaceuticals. This company, in turn, buys 32 percent of everything you sell.

You have met Mr. Woods. He is a rough, tough, aggressive, highly successful individual who has personally built his business up. He is an arch-conservative, which makes you wonder a little about his relationship with his son.

But you also know that Mr. Woods has only one son, and that is Arthur. He has stated on more than one occasion, "I've built this business to take care of my family. Some day Arthur will run it."

The reason your company—in which you have a 20 percent ownership interest—got the Woods business is because another chemical firm once brought suit against Mr. Woods' brother. Mr. Woods promptly canceled the contract, and he has never forgotten that incident.

Should your firm lose the Woods business, two things will happen: (1) Your company will be in deep financial trouble, and (2) your income, which is largely based on year-end profit-sharing bonuses, will be reduced by about 40 percent.

And yet, you are the one who has to testify in this case. You will obviously have to admit what damage was done. Whether or not you say anything about the Woods boy is another matter.

To help you play your role as the company officer, you must be fully aware of the difficulty of your position. During the trial, you cannot arbitrarily decide "to heck with the company" or forget what it would really mean to lose the business of the Woods Pharmaceutical Company. Be realistic in the role. You can do or say anything you want but only with due consideration for the consequences.

ARTHUR WOODS' STATEMENT
TO HIS ATTORNEYS

This is my report of what happened last October 17.

A group of us were having a party. We got to talking about the war in Vietnam, and a few of the guys got pretty upset about the whole thing.

We had been doing some drinking, and I think a few people were blowing grass off in a corner. Anyway, the conversation finally got around to the Flameout Company across town. Somebody said they made napalm. I've heard since that that might not be true, but we thought it was true.

Somebody said, "Why don't we go over and wreck that place?" Well, at first nobody did anything, but the talk got stronger and stronger, and the next thing I knew we all piled into our cars and drove over there.

It was dark and we only had a couple of flashlights for everybody, so I don't know exactly what happened outside. But I heard a window broken, and then we all climbed into this big office. At first, we were afraid somebody would come, but then we didn't care anymore, and we started turning things over and tearing out papers from desks.

After a few minutes, a door opened, and some guy started yelling at us. I started to head for the window, but then he stopped shouting, and everybody was laughing for some reason. But it was still pretty dark in the office, so I couldn't tell what happened. I heard one of the boys clipped the guard, though.

It wasn't long after that cops started arriving. I saw them first, outside of the window. I figured they would be coming pretty soon, anyway, so I wanted to be where I could get out in a hurry. But when I started to leave, a cop had his big face at the window, so I ducked back.

Then they came in through two different doors and the window, so there wasn't any place I could go. That same cop came in through the window, so I could see we'd had it. As a matter of fact, I just held out my hands. I mean, I was giving up. And then the guy raps me across both wrists with his club. When I ducked, he hit me across the back and knocked me down. I told him, "I quit," but all he said was, "You move just one more time and I'll split your_____ head open, boy."

Well, I didn't move. Not after that. But you should have seen what was going on in that room. There must have been thirty cops, and the kids were running all over the place, trying to get away. The cops were swinging at everybody, including the girls.

So that's what happened. But I think you ought to understand why it happened. You read all the time about this war, and what a crummy thing it is. But nobody does anything at all. Sure, the politicians wring their hands, and say how horrible it is—but they aren't over there. It's us—the kids—who have to go off and fight their wars for them. Most of us can't even vote yet.

As a matter of fact, we were talking in a political science class a few months ago about what a young person can do about the country. What it comes right down to is—nothing! If you know how to read history, you know our country is about as violent as they come. Starting with the Indians, we've been pushing people around since the day one. And, any time a young person even questions things like war, or racism, or poverty, we get told to shut up and mind our own business.

Why, we even sent a group letter to our senator in Washington. All he did was send us a form letter back, telling us how "grand" it was we were "interested."

See, the way we look at it, the whole system is loused up. Even having you defend me is a joke. All the other kids go to trial in a bunch—just because their fathers don't have the money and the right connections. Why should it be that way?

Yes, I know that sounds ungrateful. Maybe it is. But, when you can't vote, when nobody listens to you, when all you get is platitudes and lies from the people who have the power, what alternatives do you have? What's going to make outfits like Flameout stop financing this war, unless somebody takes it into their hands to make an issue out of it? All we did was make an issue out of this thing. So, what's wrong with that? And, what other way was open to us?

Arthur Woods

FOUR SESSIONS: (30 minutes each.)

OBJECTIVE: *To enable the group to reflect in depth on some of the prevailing values in our society—those coming from parents, friends, school, community, and the church.*

Session One:

Each group member will need a pencil. Distribute to each person the page headed WHAT'S IT GOING TO TAKE?—PART I, including Racial Prejudice, World Hunger, War, Pollution, Population Growth (pages 66-67). Describe the procedure and answer questions about it.

You may wish to demonstrate the procedure by putting the letters (a) through (g) on the board or on newsprint and asking for two or three responses to be sure that everyone understands how the ranking is to be done.

Give the group the entire period to complete the questionnaire and collect papers at the end of the class time. Explain that you will make charts of the results for discussion in the next session.

Between Sessions:

Prepare charts on newsprint or light cardboard and record the numbers chosen beside each letter on the chart. For example:

RACIAL PREJUDICE

a 5 1 1 3 1 7 5 (all the first choices)
b 3
c 1
d 4
e 7
f 2
g 6

On the basis of their first choices, three members of this class of seven young people considered "Deeply desirous of the good of other people" to be the most important trait in overcoming racial prejudice. Two thought "Sensitive and responsive to the feelings of others," was the most important.

After the responses of your group are charted and you talk about them together, priorities and reaction will become clear to you and to them.

Make a list of traits (1-7) on newsprint.

Session Two:

1. Return questionnaires to the group.
2. Post the list of traits where everyone can see it.
3. Present the charts, one at a time.
4. Ask: "What were your reasons for ranking various traits in different ways?"
5. For each problem area, like Racial Prejudice, ask, "What do you see as the significance of the rank order?"

Session Three:

1. Briefly review the previous session—how the group rank-ordered various questions and what they thought the rank ordering meant.
2. Post the list of traits prepared for session two.
3. Distribute copies of questions about school, family, friends, church to each person (page 68).
4. Let the group spend the rest of the session completing the questionnaires, working individually. Explain that you will make rank order charts for the next session.

Between Sessions:

1. Tally up scores for individual questions.
2. Summarize scores for school, family, and friends.
3. Compare summary score against summary of answers given to question 9.

Session Four:

1. Review what has been done, emphasizing that the work done in session three concerns what various parts of society, including the family, are *saying* about the relative importance of various traits. Racial prejudice, world hunger, war, etc., are problems we face. If we find a big difference between the traits called for to solve the problems named and the traits that school, parents, and friends (or church) want to develop in us, then our priorities are working against the solution of our problems.
2. Show the results as computed between sessions. Discuss the following questions:
What differences are there and *why?*
How do we feel about these differences?
What can we do about the differences in priorities?
What about the "practicality" of religion?

WHAT'S IT GOING TO TAKE?— PART I

Seven character traits are listed below. Most people would agree that all are desirable. Most would also agree that few people have all seven at once. We tend to be more of one thing, less of another.

Consider the relative importance of each of these traits in solving some of the serious problems now facing the world. Three of these problems—race, poverty, and war—are as old as mankind. Two others —pollution and overpopulation—are relatively new.

Your job is to decide which of the seven traits are most important in solving each of these problems, and *in what order*. This may not be easy. Your first reaction might be simply to say, "They are all equally important," but your job here is to discriminate between them in order of importance. You need to decide which of the seven traits is most important for solving, say, racial prejudice, which is second most important, which is third, etc.

Here are the seven traits. Each is numbered:

1. Deeply desirous of the good of other people.

2. Committed to the loftiest ideals possible.

3. Intelligent, knowledgeable, well-informed.

4. Practical, able to cope with and solve problems.

5. Sensitive and responsive to the feelings of others.

6. Energetic and hard-working.

7. Firm believer in God.

Think about these seven traits. Now think about *racial prejudice and class discrimination,* and what these words mean to you. Which one of the seven traits would be most helpful in overcoming the problem of racial prejudice? Put the number of that trait beside the letter (a) under "Racial Prejudice."

Which trait would come next? Put that number beside the letter (b). Go on until you have ranked all seven traits in the order of their importance to you *in relation to the problem of racial prejudice.*

Do the same thing with "World Hunger," "War," "Pollution," and "Population Growth." Take your time.

RACIAL PREJUDICE

Racial prejudice and class discrimination are causing serious trouble in our country. These problems would best be resolved if all people possessed the following traits, in the following order of importance:

a.

b.

c.

d.

e.

f.

g.

WORLD HUNGER

"Of the 3.5 billion people in the world, at least 500 million are undernourished, and another billion malnourished. Every 8.6 seconds someone dies from starvation." (Hugh Moore Fund.) The primary reason is simply that these people have no money to buy food (or anything else). This problem might be solved if all of us possessed the following traits, in the following order of importance:

a.

b.

c.

d.

e.

f.

g.

WAR

Man has always fought wars. No wars have been more violent, bloody, or frequent than those of the twentieth century. We might see peace in the next century if all people possessed the following traits, in the following order of importance:

a.

b.

c.

d.

e.

f.

g.

POLLUTION

There is no question but that we are poisoning our atmosphere and water, all over the earth. Some ecologists tell us we may even kill all life in the next twenty-five years if nothing is done. More would be done faster if all people possessed the following traits, in the following order of importance:

a.

b.

c.

d.

e.

f.

g.

POPULATION GROWTH

Although the rate of population growth is slowing down, even the present rate will, in about a century, result in the people of the earth weighing more than the earth itself; an obviously impossible situation. This problem would best be solved if all people possessed the following traits, in the following order of importance:

a.

b.

c.

d.

e.

f.

g.

WHAT'S IT GOING TO TAKE?—
PART II

SCHOOL

You spend a lot of time in school. As far as you have been able to figure out, which are the traits your school is most concerned with developing, in their order of importance?

a.

b.

c.

d.

e.

f.

g.

FAMILY

Much of your remaining time is spent with your family. Considering your parents, which traits do they seem to feel are most important for you to develop, in the order of importance?

a.

b.

c.

d.

e.

f.

g.

FRIENDS

And you also spend a good deal of time with friends. As you reflect on it, which traits do your friends seem to hold in highest esteem—which do they respect—in order of importance?

a.

b.

c.

d.

e.

f.

g.

CHURCH

Finally, you spend a small proportion of your time in church. Whatever you think of "church" and religious matters, how would you say the church ranks these traits, in order of importance?

a.

b.

c.

d.

e.

f.

g.

Religious
Belief

TWO TO THREE SESSIONS: (45 minutes each.)

OBJECTIVE: *To motivate the group to consider more deeply the source of their religious beliefs and to contrast these with the sources of their other beliefs.*

Session One:

1. Hand a copy of CALCUTTA—PART I (page 72) to each member of the group and allow everyone 10 minutes to complete it.

2. Discuss the answers *briefly*. Check by show of hands to see how many answered the yes-no questions. For questions 3, 5, 7, 9, 10 check quickly which ones they answered.

3. Ask the group to change the word "Calcutta" to "God" on the questionnaire and complete it a second time.

4. Begin discussing their answers. In the next session you will have a more detailed discussion. Collect the questionnaires at the end of the session.

Session Two:

1. Continue discussion of group members' answers to the questionnaire. In response to their statements ask: *"But, how do you know?"*

2. Pass out copies of CALCUTTA—PART II (page 73), and have each person answer the three questions. Collect the completed questionnaires at the end of the session.

Session Three (or in Session Two if there is time):

1. Have members share what differences there were in their answers to questions 1 and 2.

2. Ask them to read or explain their reasons for giving different answers (question 3).

3. How do you think other people (for example your parents, friends) feel about these questions? Why?

4. Why do you think people fight belief in God?

1. Do you believe there is a Calcutta, India?
   _____Yes
   _____No

2. Are you fairly certain there is a Calcutta, India?
   _____Yes
   _____No

3. Check *all* of the following which have provided you with this confidence:
   _____I have read about Calcutta.
   _____People have told me there is a Calcutta.
   _____I've seen Calcutta. (Personally, not on TV)

4. If you have read about Calcutta, do you have positive, certain *proof* that those who did the writing are not either wrong, or lying, or both?
   _____Yes, I do have such proof.
   _____No, I don't have such proof.

5. If you still trust these written sources, why? (Check *all* of the answers that you agree with.)
   _____They have nothing to gain by lying about Calcutta.
   _____They seem to have told the truth about other things, so I conclude they are being truthful about this.
   _____The writers say they have seen Calcutta, or know others who have.
   _____The writing sounds as if it were done by men or women who are sane, so I conclude they are being sane when they claim there is a Calcutta.

6. If other people have told you there is a Calcutta, do you have certain, absolute proof they aren't either wrong, or lying?
   _____Yes, I do have such proof.
   _____No, I don't have such proof.

7. If you trust those who have told you about Calcutta, then why? (Check all answers you agree with.)
   _____They have nothing to gain by lying to me.
   _____They don't usually lie about other things, so I'll trust them about this.

   _____They say they've seen Calcutta, or know others who have.
   _____They seem sane enough and so I conclude they are being sensible about Calcutta.

8. If you haven't personally seen Calcutta, and *no matter how sure you are it exists,* can you *prove* it exists, without actually seeing it?
   _____Yes
   _____No

9. If you can't prove there is a Calcutta, how would you "classify" your belief that it exists? (Choose *one* of the three classifications below.)
   _____My belief that there is a Calcutta is a matter of *proven, factual knowledge,* identical to my belief that nuclear energy exists, even though I haven't seen it.
   _____My belief that there is a Calcutta is a matter of *reasoning.* I have applied logic and the scientific method, and have reached a theory that Calcutta "must" exist.
   _____My belief that there is a Calcutta is a matter of *faith.* I can't prove it. I haven't seen it. But, I still believe it exists, and I believe so very strongly.

10. Suppose you were to read in a newspaper (one that you trust, by the way) that six out of every ten people in the world claim there is no such thing as a Calcutta. What would be your *most likely* reaction? (Choose *only one.*)
    _____I would say that six out of every ten people in the world have flipped their lids for some reason.
    _____I would begin to wonder about those who have told me there is a Calcutta. I might not change my mind, but I would be a little more skeptical.
    _____I would probably change my mind and decide there was no Calcutta. Six out of ten people in a world this big means over two billion people don't agree with me. I must be wrong.

1. It is reasonable to assume that the vast majority of people who believe in Calcutta, India, do so for reasons pretty much like your own. How would you describe this belief?

   ———It is very naïve and silly.

   ———It is somewhat naïve and silly.

   ———It is somewhat reasonable.

   ———It is quite reasonable.

2. It is reasonable to assume that the vast majority of people who believe in God do so for reasons pretty similar to your own—*and* for pretty much the same reasons they believe in Calcutta. How would you describe this belief?

   ———It is very naïve and silly.

   ———It is somewhat naïve and silly.

   ———It is somewhat reasonable.

   ———It is quite reasonable.

3. If there is *any* difference between the answers you checked off above, use the rest of this page, and the back of the page if necessary, to state *why* this difference exists.

ONE SESSION: (50 minutes.)

OBJECTIVE: *To have the group move to a broader understanding of why Christianity defines man's selfishness as the most common form of idolatry.*

Before this session write one of the twenty-two questions from pages 76-78 separately on the top half of an 8½ x 11 inch sheet of plain white paper (that is, one question to a sheet). Label each (Q 1), (Q 2), etc. Draw a horizontal line across each sheet and below the line write (A 1), (A 2) to correspond with each Q number. DO NOT WRITE IN THE ANSWERS.

On the back of each sheet put a large number 1, 2, 3, etc., corresponding with the question number on the other side.

Provide a fine-point dark-color felt-tip pen for each group member.

It would be helpful in this session to have everyone sit around a table or on the floor in order to write.

To begin the session hand out a felt-tip pen and a sheet headed WORDS AND DEEDS (see page 75) to each member of the group and give everyone a few moments to read the material on the sheet.

Before starting the discussion, make sure everyone understands the definitions used. Say that they do not necessarily have to *agree* with the definitions—they simply need to understand them, so they can apply them in the ensuing discussion.

Explain the procedure. Place questions 1 to 11 face down in the center of the group. Have each person pick one up. (If there are extras, pick them up yourself.) Ask them *NOT* to read the questions yet. Now begin with the person who has question 1, asking him or her to turn it over, read it aloud, and point to another group member to answer. When a correct answer is given, the person holding question 1 writes the answer on the bottom half of the sheet beside (A 1).

Each time, the person who is reading a question should point to someone who hasn't already answered a question. If the person asked doesn't have an answer, anyone in the group can give an answer.

Continue this process rapidly, and then have all eleven sheets posted, in order, on the wall for the group to read through silently and quickly.

Repeat the process with questions 12 through 22.

Ask as a final question for general discussion:

"The church says that the *real* cause of war, poverty, hunger, prejudice, and all of our other problems is a thing called 'selfishness.' As we have defined it, selfishness is the most common form of idolatry—worshiping the wrong god. Do you think this view is correct, or justified?"

Often the trouble with talking about subjects like "god," "religion," and "worship" is that those terms are so broad and general that each person in the conversation is using a different definition of the word.

You cannot discuss these subjects unless you first agree on what the words mean. Therefore, for purposes of our discussion today, we will use the following definitions. These definitions are not complete, or entirely correct. However, we will use them so that we will have common definitions for our discussion.

1. *GOD*   That single thing or goal which is most important to a given person; which is the primary purpose or motive for that person; what the person most worships in life.

2. *RELIGION*   What a person believes about his or her particular "god"; what that god is like in the person's thoughts.

3. *WORSHIP*   What a person does about his or her god; how the person behaves toward it and applies his or her religion in daily life.

Now, given these definitions (and remembering that they are quite narrow) it would be theoretically possible to determine what you or another person has for a "god" or "religion" simply by observing your particular form of "worship"—that is, by observing what a person DOES MOST, you can deduce who or what that person's real "god" is.

For example, a boy or girl who spends all of his or her time thinking about some other boy or girl, and whose actions are almost entirely directed toward that other boy or girl, has, for the moment, set that other person up as a "god."

QUESTIONS	POSSIBLE ANSWERS (in parentheses are extra explanations)

(Q 1) What does "idolatry" mean?

(A 1) *Worshiping false gods.*
(As defined by Christianity: worshiping any god other than the One True God.)

(Q 2) According to the definitions we are using, how could you tell if a person was idolatrous?

(A 2) *Primarily by what the person does—by his or her form of worship.*
(The most important objects or goals of this behavior would be the person's "idol." If the focus of this behavior, or "worship," is anything other than God, then the person is idolatrous.)

(Q 3) What does "sacrifice" mean?

(A 3) *Giving up something.*

(Q 4) What things do people sometimes have to sacrifice?

(A 4) *Time*
Effort, or energy
Talent, skills, etc.
Money and material possessions
Life itself

(Q 5) Can you avoid sacrificing these things?

(A 5) *No.*
(Unless you sit and do nothing all day, and even then, you are sacrificing time.)

(Q 6) How, then, might you redefine "worship" in terms of sacrifice?

(A 6) *Worship could be defined as how you sacrifice your time, efforts, talents, money, and life.*
(They must be sacrificed anyway. Your form of worship is how you sacrifice them.)

(Q 7) What or who is the true god of a person who spends most of his time, energy, etc., making money?

(A 7) *In fact, this person's real god is himself. He makes money for himself.*
(At first, it looks as though money is his idol, but he makes the money for himself.)

(Q 8) What is the true god of a person who spends most of his time, energy, talents, and so forth, in buying clothes and furniture?

(A 8) *Again what this person really worships is himself.*
(Even though it looks as though the things are what he worships.)

(Q 9) What is the true god of a politician who spends most of his time and effort seeking more power?

(A 9) *The politician who does this is worshiping himself. He is his real god.*
(Again, not "power" itself.)

(Q 10) What would the "religion" of these people be?

(A 10) *Their religion is what they believe about themselves.*
(As defined in the paper, the religion of these people would be what they believe about their real god.)

(Q 11) Would this be the case if they didn't think they were nice people? If they didn't "like" themselves?

(A 11) *It would still be their religion.*
(According to the definition, there is no question about whether religious beliefs are positive or negative, good or bad.)
(The definition simply says that a person's true religion is what that person believes about the god he or she really worships.)

(Q 12) Is what these people believe about the God of Christianity their religion?

(A 12) *No, not according to the definitions given.*
(Their beliefs about the God of Christianity are only that—beliefs.)
(Their "religious beliefs" are limited, by definition, to what they believe about themselves, since they worship themselves.)

(Q 13) Is what they believe about the God of Christianity particularly important?

(A 13) *Presumably not, since they are merely intellectual beliefs.*
(Their important beliefs are the ones which, for them, are "religious"—the ones they have concerning themselves.)

(Q 14) What is really meant, then, by the statement you hear nowadays: "Religion doesn't have any meaning any more."

(A14) *That statement means that people's beliefs about God don't make much difference.*
(But this is the case because their beliefs about God are not their real religion.)

(Q 15) According to Christian belief, who rules the universe?

(A 15) *God.*

(Q 16) What is the word we use to define those who try to overthrow rulers?

(A 16) *Rebels.*

(Q 17) According to these definitions, what is a person who puts self in the place of God as the object of worship?

(A 17) *A rebel against God, since the person is trying to be his or her own ruler.*

(Q 18) What must the rebel do if the rightful ruler is to regain power?

(A 18) *Give up—surrender.*

(Q 19) What will cause this to happen?

(A 19) *One of two things:*
—Either God forcefully takes back the power.
—Or else the rebel must admit to being wrong.

(Q 20) What is the word we use to define "admitting you are wrong"?

(A 20) *Repentance.*

(Q 21) Now, in real life, how would a person act out a surrender to God? (In terms of the three words defined in your paper.)

(A 21) *The person would accept God as the real god— the central purpose of his or her life.*
(Doing this would automatically make the person's beliefs about God his or her "religion," since your religion is what you believe about the one thing most important to you.)
(Would redirect the person's actions—his or her "worship"—toward doing what God wants, rather than what the person wants.)

(Q 22) Have you noticed many people acting this way?

(A 22) *No.*
(It is not a very universal characteristic.)

THREE SESSIONS: (45 minutes each.)

OBJECTIVE: *To stimulate group members to think about and clearly articulate their views on the basis of religious beliefs.*

Session One: Allow 20 minutes for steps 1 through 6.

1. Tell the group that you will be having a debate to see how many ideas they can generate and how well they can hear each other's point of view.

2. Write on newsprint the following proposition:

"RELIGIOUS BELIEFS ARE THE PRODUCT OF WISHFUL THINKING."

3. Have the group divide into pairs. Each pair has 5 minutes to prepare a one-sentence statement describing what they think the proposition means.

4. Have each pair read their statement and a leader write it(in abbreviated form if that is possible without changing what is being said) under the proposition.

5. On another newsprint sheet write:

Agree   Tend to agree   Tend to disagree   Disagree

By show of hands have group members indicate how they respond to the *proposition*.

6. Divide group in half—one group to disagree and one group to agree. Use your judgment in doing this. As much as possible, have individuals work where they placed themselves on the scale. To have the group divide evenly, those who seem only to tend to agree may move to disagree and vice versa.

If almost all (or all) members agree or disagree initially, ask for those who can think of points on the other side to shift for purposes of a debate. Let them know that one object for each debating team is to come up with as *many* points as possible, and that it is a challenge to their brain power.

7. Have the teams work in separate locations so that they will not be distracted by each other. If there are two adult leaders, one works with each team. A leader working alone moves back and forth between the teams.

8. The first task of each member of both teams is to complete SHEET C individually (see page 80).

9. Each team then lists on newsprint all the points the team members have listed under (2) on SHEET C. Combining points that fit together, come up with one newsprint list of as many *different* points as possible. Have the team keep this list.

10. The team divides into pairs and each pair prepares to present one or more points in the debate with the other team. Encourage the teams to work hard to get enough points for each pair to have at least one to work on.

Session Two: Round One of the Debate

1. Teams meet as pairs and finish working on their preparation of a 2- to 3-minute presentation. One member of each pair will be the spokesman for the pair in round one.

2. Have teams sit in rows facing each other with the spokesman for each pair facing the spokesman of a pair from the other team. The partner of each spokesman sits directly behind that spokesman, so that there are two rows of one team facing two rows of the other team.

3. Each team member needs a pencil and paper.

4. An adult leader keeps time. Each spokesman has 2 to 3 minutes. He or she speaks directly to the person opposite. All members of the opposing team write down what point or points they hear made by the speaker.

5. Have each spokesman present one or more points —alternating sides, first agree, then disagree.

6. Immediately have teams huddle and using their notes made in the debate have them make a newsprint list of all the points made by the opposing team.

7. Have each team post their original list of points and compare it to the list *heard* by their opponents.

Whichever team has the more accurate list of points *heard* is ahead for round one.

8. Have the teams separate so that each pair can prepare a rebuttal of the points made by the pair sitting opposite them. In the rebuttal round the other member of the pair is to make the presentation.

Session Three: Round Two of the Debate

1. Have the pairs finish preparing for their rebuttal presentation.

2. Each team makes a newsprint list of all the points they will be making in the rebuttal in the order in which they will be presented.

3. Repeat steps 4, 5, 6, 7 in round one.

4. Looking at all the points listed as made by teams in both rounds, discuss the question: "What have we learned by having this debate?"

SHEET C
RELIGIOUS BELIEFS

PROPOSITION: "Religious beliefs are the product of wishful thinking."

(1) Develop one or more examples—examples drawn from real life, if you wish—to illustrate your side of the debate. (For instance an example of somebody who was—or was not—engaging in wishful thinking when it came to religious beliefs.)

(2) List below two or three specific points to support your side of the proposition.